Mandragora
King of India

by Nirjay Mahindru

T0347786

Director **Jatinder Verma**
Designer **Claudia Mayer**
Lighting Designer **Jonathan Clark**
Music **Chandran Veyattummal**
Production and Stage Manager **John Page**
Publicity Design **Simon Williams**
Costume Supervisor **Claire Hardaker**
Marketing **Ben Jefferies** for **Guy Chapman Associates**
PR **David Bloom** for **Guy Chapman Associates**
Audience Development **Suman Bhuchar**

First performed at Tron Theatre, Glasgow, Thursday 22 April 2004

Tara Arts
Artistic Director **Jatinder Verma**
Associate Director **Claudia Mayer**
Consultant General Manager **Gareth Johnson**
Trainee General Manager **Stefanie Huter**
Administrator **Nirjay Mahindru**
IT Support **Hitesh Chauhan**
Finance Officer **Marcus Duntoye**

Tara Arts, 356 Garratt Lane, London SW18 4ES
Tel 020 8333 4457, www.tara-arts.com

Cast

Jasper, Lord Hastings	**James Bellorini**
King Mandragora, Spade	**Antony Bunsee**
Thatch, Lord Munshi	**Marc Elliott**
Bindio, Lord Susna	**Arif Javid**
Sunita	**Dina Mousawi**
Lady Catherine, Psychic	**Katie Pattinson**

There will be one interval of twenty minutes.

Smoking in the auditorium is not permitted.
Please ensure that mobile phones, pagers and digital alarm watches are **switched off** before you enter the auditorium.

Biographies

James Bellorini Jasper, Hastings

James studied at Dartington College of Arts, followed by a year performing and directing with a French street-theatre company. His acting work includes: *147* (Oval House); *Under the Earth*, *Metamorphosis* and *House of Desires* (BAC); *East* (Vaudeville Theatre); *Nirvana* (Riverside Studios); *Epitaph for the Whales*, *The Puppetmaster* and *A Box of Bananas* (The Gate Theatre); *L'Arte della Commedia* (The Old Vic); *The Merchant of Venice* and *A Christmas Carol* (Palace Theatre, Westcliff); *Woyzeck* (UK National Tour); *Red Noses* (Oxford Playhouse); *The Bald Prima Donna* (Young Vic Studio); *Le Pub* (National Theatre); *EastEnders* (BBC TV); *A Film for Radio* (BBC Radio 4).

Antony Bunsee King Mandragora, Spade

Antony was born in London and brought up in Salisbury. He trained at Bristol Old Vic Theatre School.

Recent theatre: Archangel Gabriel in *Paradise Lost* (Northampton); the title role in *Dracula* (Derby Playhouse); Tai in *Midnight's Children* (RSC); Hamidullah in *Passage to India* (Shared Experience); Quri Shah in *Homebody/Kabul* (Young Vic/Cheek by Jowl).

Previous theatre work with Tara Arts includes: Puck in *Midsummer Night's Dream*; *Pinocchio goes Asia*; *Oedipus*; *The Government Inspector*.

Marc Elliott Thatch, Lord Munshi

Marc made his professional debut with the RSC as Lucius in *Julius Caesar* and went on to play roles in *A Winter's Tale* and *Macbeth*. He was in the world premiere of Nigel Williams' *Lord of the Flies* at The Other Place, in which he played Jack. His theatre credits include: *Two Lost Souls on a Dirty Night*; *The Mill on the Floss*; *Still Lives*; *Romeo and Juliet*; *Les Liaisons Dangereuses*. Marc most recently took the role of Jean in NAACH Theatre Company's production of *Miss Julie*.

For radio, he has recorded parts in *The Mob* (BBC World Service) and *Jadoo!* (BBC Radio 4). He made his television debut this year in *Mile High*.

Arif Javid Bindio, Lord Susna

Arif Javid trained at the London drama studio in Ealing. He began his acting career working in young people's theatre with companies like Quicksilver, Breakout and The Oily Cart.

His recent theatre credits include the parts of Salim in a national tour of *My Beautiful Laundrette* and Indra in *The Ramayana* (Birmingham Rep).

He has appeared in numerous TV dramas including *A Sense of Guilt* with Trevor Eve; *EastEnders*; *The Bill*; *Casualty*; *Hornblower* (during the making of which, as a member of the Magic Circle, he entertained the vast crowds of visitors with his cabaret magic act). He can be seen at the moment as the taxi driver Ali Aslam in the new medical soap drama *Kismet Road* (Community Channel).

His film credits include: *My Son the Fanatic*.

Arif is very pleased to be appearing in this, his first Tara Arts theatre production.

Dina Mousawi Sunita

Dina is very pleased to be working with Tara Arts again, after appearing in Tara's epic trilogy *Journey to the West* (2002). Other theatre credits include: *When Amar Met Jay* (UK tour, Hangama Productions); *Introduction to Shakespeare, Shakespeare and Tragedy, The Breakfast Show (*Big Wheel TIE, European Tour); *West Side Story* (Alhambra Theatre, Bradford); *Oklahoma* (Edinburgh Fringe); *Seven Brides for Seven Brothers* (Edinburgh Fringe), *The King and I* (Alhambra Theatre, Bradford).

Television credits include: *Cold Feet* (Granada); *Dalziel and Pascoe* (BBC); *King Girl* (BBC); *Wilderness Edge* (Granada); *Just Us* (ITV); *The Prime Minister's Brain* (ITV).

Film credits include: *Asylum* (Maximise Ltd); *King of Bollywood* (I Dream Productions).

Katie Pattinson Lady Catherine, Psychic

Katie studied at Mountview Theatre School and Cambridge University.

Most recent theatre credits include a national tour of *Jane Eyre* (Good Company). Prior to that Katie spent most of 2002 at the Theatre by the Lake, Keswick, where she appeared in *The Good Companions*, *All My Sons* and Charlotte Jones' *In Flame*. Other theatre work includes repertory, West End, national and international tours to theatres from Hong Kong to Belfast and the Arctic Circle to Madrid!

Theatre credits include: *A Penny for a Song* (Oxford Stage Company); *The Tempest* (Salisbury Playhouse); *Macbeth* (Hull Truck); the world premiere of *Mushroom Man* (Hungry Grass Theatre Company); *A Streetcar Named Desire* and *A Christmas Carol* (American Drama Group Europe); *Romeo and Juliet* and *Macbeth* (Box Clever Theatre Company); *Penthisilea* and *Family* (New End Theatre).

TV and film credits include: *Crimewatch*, *Thunderpants*.

Nirjay Mahindru Writer

Nirjay Mahindru was born in Birmingham. He studied Politics and Modern History at Manchester University and then attended Cygnet Training Theatre Drama School in Exeter. He was a professional actor for over 12 years before moving into theatre administration. Mandragora, King of India was his first play. His second, *Felling the Cedar Mountain* (2002) won a new playwriting competition and is optioned for production by Tara Arts. His third play *Distortion* (2003) received a development commission from Tamasha Theatre. He is one of the writers for the BBC's new Asian Radio Soap *Silver Street*. He recently founded Conspirator's Kitchen theatre company. He lives in London with his wife and two children.

Jatinder Verma Director

Artistic Director and co-founder of Tara Arts (in 1977), Jatinder has written, adapted and directed most of Tara's productions, from reinventing the classics of both the European and the Indian sub-continental canon to devised pieces and new writing, developing a characteristic 'Binglish' performance style.

In 1990, he became the first director from among Britain's migrant communities to be invited to stage a play at the Royal National Theatre – his own adaptation of Moliere's Tartuffe – which he produced with an all-Asian cast. The success of this production was followed by The Little Clay Cart and Cyrano de Bergerac, both for the RNT.

Jatinder was awarded a Time Out/01 for London Special Award for his contribution to the bonding of British, European and Asian cultures and Honorary Doctorates by De Montfort, Leicester and Exeter Universities.

Awards: 1990 – Time/01 For London Special Award for 'his outstanding contribution through both Tara Arts and the National Theatre to the London theatre scene and the bonding of British, Asian and European cultures'; Asian City Club Arts and Achievement Award. 2001 – Asian 2001 Achievers Award for Culture.

Media: A regular contributor to radio and TV for both arts and current affairs programmes, Jatinder has also written and presented a variety of programmes.

Radio Documentaries: Ashes to the Ganges (1997 BBC Radio 4), winner of a Sony Award and a CRE Race & Media Award; *The Nine Cities of Delhi* (1998 BBC Radio 4); *The Great Sentinel and the Great Soul* (1998 BBC Radio 4), documentary on the relationship of Tagore and Gandhi; *A Nation of Shopkeepers* (1999 BBC Radio 4); *A Southall Lad* (2000 BBC Radio 4), documentary on the murder of Gurdeep Singh Chaggar in Southall in 1976; *Asian Diasporas* (2002 BBC Radio 4 & World Service) a three-part examination of the diverse Asian diaspora around the globe; *New Country, New Life* (2003 BBC Radio 4) a three-part examination of refugees in three continents.

Radio Drama: The Dreams of Tipu Sultan by Girish Karnad, (1997 BBC Radio 4); *The Little Clay Cart* adapted by Jatinder Verma (1997 BBC World Service); *The Cyclist* by Vijay Tendulkar (1998 BBC World Service).

Television: The Shape of the Heart, a Migrant's Tale (1996 BBC TV for the OU); *Antony and Cleopatra* (1999 BBC TV for the OU)

Publications: 'The Challenge of Binglish', chapter in *Analysing Performance*, ed. Patrick Campbell, Manchester University Press (1996); 'In Contact with the Gods', chapter in *Directors Talk Theatre*, ed. Maria M Delgado & Paul Heritage, Manchester University Press (1996); 'Binglishing the Stage: a Generation of Asian Theatre in England', chapter in *Theatre Matters*, ed. Richard Boon & Jane Plastow, Cambridge University Press (1998); 'Mourning Diana, Asian style', chapter in *Mourning Diana: Nation, Culture and the Performance of Grief*, ed. Adrian Kear & Deborah Lynn Steinberg, Routledge (1999); 'Sorry, No Saris!', chapter in *Theatre in a Cool Climate*, ed. Vera Gottlieb and Colin Chambers, Amber Lane Press (2000)

A frequent speaker at conferences in Britain and overseas, he is also regularly invited to give lectures and workshops in universities and drama colleges.

Lectures: Royal Society of Arts, UK – Sir George Birdwood Lecture, 1989, *Transformations in Culture: The Asian in Britain*; Portland State University, Oregon, USA – Inaugural Lecture, 1994, *Border Crossings*; First Asian Theatre Conference, Birmingham, UK – Keynote Speech, 1994, *Historical Developments and Contemporary Identity of Asian Theatre*; Inter-Cult Conference, Stockholm, Sweden, 1996, *The challenge of theatre in a multicultural Europe*; Standing Conference of University Drama Departments, Scarborough, UK – Keynote Speech, 1996, *A jungli approach to interculturalism*; Conference on Asian Writing, Oldham, UK, 1996, *Asian Writing in English*; Cumberland Lodge, Windsor, UK, 1997, *Asian Agenda for British Public Policy: the role of the Media*; New Stages Conference, Oslo – Keynote Speech, 2001, *The history and impact of cultural diversity on theatre and the performing arts in the UK*; 'Peshkar' Conference, Oldham – Keynote Speech, 2001, *Are We Visible? – A survey of Asian Arts post-September 11*; Watermans DNAsia Conference, London – Keynote Speech, 2003, *Asian Arts in the 21st Century*.

Claudia Mayer Designer

Claudia Mayer studied with Percy Harris at the Motley Design Course. Before joining Tara in 1998, she worked as a freelance designer for theatre, ballet and opera.

Opera and Ballet includes work for Wilton's Music Hall, The Birmingham Royal Ballet, Broomhill Opera, The Royal Opera House, English Touring Opera, Pimlico Opera, Garden Venture, British Youth Opera.

Theatre work has included the Royal Court Theatre, The Young Vic, The Gate Theatre, The Ambassadors Theatre, Sadlers Wells, Riverside Studios and several other London venues.

Regional work includes The Lyceum Theatre, Edinburgh, The West Yorkshire Playhouse, Leeds, Theatre Clwyd, Mold, The Playhouse Theatre, Liverpool, The Crucible Theatre, Sheffield, The Library Theatre, Manchester, The Octagon Theatre, Bolton, The Gateway Theatre, Chester and several other regional theatres.

She has also worked with Oxford Stage Company, 7:84 England, Monstrous Regiment, Pip Simmons Theatre Group, Joint Stock, Foco Novo, The London Theatre Ensemble, Mrs Worthington's Daughters, and many other fringe and touring companies.

For Tara: *Dance Like a Man*; *Exodus, Genesis, Revelations, 2001, a Ramayan Odyssey, Journey to the West (a trilogy), A Taste for Mangoes*.

Jonathan Clark Lighting Designer

Recent lighting design includes: *Gone To Earth* for Shared Experience, Lyric Hammersmith and Tour; *The Tale That Wags The Dog* for Drum Theatre, Plymouth; *Boxbeat* for Zoo Nation at The Place, London; *Maverick Matador* for Juliet Aster at Dance East; *Mountains are Mountains* for Phillipp Gehmacher at Tanz Quartier, Vienna and European tour; *Underworld* for Frantic Assembly at the Lyric Hammersmith and Tour; *Embryonic Dreams* for Pyromania at The Pleasance; *A Colliers Friday Night* for ODS at Battersea Arts Centre.

Recent re-lights includes: *The Taming of The Shrew* for Plymouth Theatre Royal and Thelma Holt Ltd; *After Mrs.Rochester, A Passage To India, The Clearing* and *The Magic Toyshop* for Shared Experience; *This Is Our Youth* at The Garrick Theatre, London; *Tosca & Nabucco* for The Moldovan National Opera; *Plunge & Undone* for Scottish Dance Theatre; *Sell Out* and *Hymns* for Frantic Assembly, West End, UK and International tours.

Recent production credits includes: *The Goat or Who is Sylvia* at the Apollo Theatre, London. Grange Park Opera 2003, *Vagina Monologues* and *Gagarin Way* at the Arts Theatre, London; *Caledonian Rd* and *Ghost Ward*, site specific projects for the Almeida Theatre; *Mapping the Edge* for wilson+wilson company at the Sheffield Crucible and site specific.

Chandran Veyattummal Music

V Chandran trained as a classical Indian musician. Chandran has worked extensively in theatre and TV as musician and composer. He has been a member of Footsbarn Theatre Company in France for the past eight years. He last worked with Tara on the company's production for the Royal National Theatre of *The Little Clay Cart* and last year's *A Taste for Mangoes* at Wiltons Music Hall. He is an Associate Artist for Tara.

John Page Production and Stage Manager

After forming his own Theatre Company at the age of 11, based in a double garage in Wiltshire, John went to train at Central School of Speech and Drama.

His recent work includes production management for Peepolykus Theatre Company (UK and International Tours of *Let the Donkey Go, Goose Nights, I am A Coffee, Horses for Courses*; 1996 – 2000); *The David Strassman Show* (Apollo Theatre and UK Tour 1997); for The Production Desk: Athol Fugard's *The Island* (Old Vic, UK Tour, 2000) and the acclaimed Wiltons Music Hall production of *Yiimimangaliso / The Mysteries* (Wiltons & and UK Tour 2002).

He has also toured to Croatia, Cyprus, India, Bangladesh and most of Europe. This is his third project for Tara Arts.

Claire Hardaker Costume Supervisor

Claire studied English Literature at Durham University and Arts Foundation at Bradford College (BTEC). Currently she is in her final year at London College of Fashion, studying BA (Hons) Costume, Make-up and Technical effects for the Performing Arts, specialising in costume.

So far Claire has been involved in: *The Caucasian Chalk Circle* at the Alhambra Studio, Bradford (Puppet Construction); *Bradford Carnival* (Costume Construction); BBC *Music Live* (Costume Construction); *Die Fledermaus* with English Touring Opera (Assistant Supervisor); BBC – *Christmas at the Club Blue Peter* (Costume Construction); *Six Characters in Search of an Author*, UCL Drama Society (Costume design & Supervisor); *The Tragic Comedy of Transistor Boy and Other Stories* directed by Netia Jones at the Cochrane Theatre (Costume Designer).

And some things that should not have been forgotten were lost,
History became legend, legend became myth.

JRR Tolkien, *Lord of the Rings*

First published in 2004 by Oberon Books Ltd
(incorporating Absolute Classics)
521 Caledonian Road, London N7 9RH
Tel: +44 (0) 20 7607 3637 / Fax: +44 (0) 20 7607 3629
e-mail: info@oberonbooks.com
www.oberonbooks.com

A catalogue record for this book is available from the British
Library.

PB ISBN: 978-1-84002-445-6
E ISBN: 978-1-78319-476-6

Cover image: Simon Williams Design (www.simonwilliams.co.uk)

Printed in Great Britain by Antony Rowe Ltd, Chippenham.
eBook conversion by Replika Press Pvt. Ltd, India.

Visit www.oberonbooks.com to read more about all our books
and to buy them. You will also find features, author interviews and
news of any author events, and you can sign up for e-newsletters
so that you're always first to hear about our new releases.

Characters in order of appearance

SPADE
A Soldier (Private)

JASPER
Lieutenant to the King

SUSNA
Lord of Madras

MANDRAGORA
King of India

LORD MUNSHI
Chief Council to the King

PSYCHIC
A Soothsayer

SUNITA
The Daughter of Bindio

BINDIO
A Poet. Father to Sunita

THATCH
Lord of Lincolnshire

HASTINGS
Leader of the Britannic party

CATHERINE
Lady of Kent and fiancée to Hastings

PROLOGUE

Have Trust in those fertile imaginations I'm sure you pos-
    sess in abundance,
Think back to a time far off now, a hazy misty past hiding
    history's shadows,
O hear the poetry good people and travel with me back
    now to that land we call India,
See it in those times past, let it clearly come to focus, hear
    the sounds, Embrace the colour and vibrancy, let it lie
    fertile in thy imaginations like a virgin waiting for her
    first taste of sexual seed,
See an Indian tableau painted with striking colours that
    shimmer in the light,
And in this state where thy sophisticated imaginations float,
For I do trust that carefully cultivated minds wait in hungry
    anticipation,
Consider me a *Maître d'* at the finest culinary establishments
    of this fair city,
I do greet you most sincerely with the false humility of our
    chef,
And offer you this night's main course, with the caveat of a
    health warning,
That the characters in this tale are real and any resem-
    blance to fictional ones is purely deliberate,
After all, good people, remember the Old Indian saying,
    'Some lies are True'.
**We therefore serve you our tale, the first part of
    the adventures and exploits of Mandragora,
    King of India!**

ACT ONE

Scene One

The port of Bombay. A stormy night. A soldier is on night watch. Another enters.

SPADE: Who goes there?

JASPER: Who asks?

SPADE: Villain! You dare ask the king's soldier questions?

JASPER: (*Laughing.*) Put up your sword!

SPADE: Noble Jasper your games of folly will get you an untimely death.

JASPER: In faith good Spade, I am wont to meet it with a smile on my face. For 'tis said the Indians of old were like lovers at first sight when Death kissed their faces.

SPADE: How so?

JASPER Life and Death do in the same orbit travel. To rejoice in one and fear t'other is a misconception.

SPADE: Rejoice in death? That is unnatural Jasper.

JASPER: Unnatural? This brooding night that unleashes lightning and belches forth a thunderous cry, is this then natural or unnatural?

SPADE: It's nature's order.

JASPER: If 'tis natural for the Gods to scream, then why fear? Ah dear Spade, your mind imprisons you. The meaning of Life is re-incarnate and only in Death do we truly live.

SPADE: Sir, with due respect, this is no time to ponder on the philosophicals. It is a strange night. I saw peacocks flying in the night sky with their feathers on fire. They flew straight into the Qutub Minar tower, and the tower bloomed in flames. I heard the screams of people as they fell to their death and with a ravenous thunder, the tower fell to the ground. I'm sure these are symbols of the royal birth.

JASPER: This night a Prince is born.

SPADE: Is it a boy? Have you been to Court?

JASPER: I attend the King tomorrow.

SPADE: If the child's a boy, the stars promise he'll be a lion, endowered with a mighty roar.

Thunder is heard.

SPADE: Listen to the Gods Sir. Maybe the umbilical chord is cut and the little lion roars!

Enter Lord SUSNA in an agitated state.

SUSNA: Is that the Kybalian warrior Jasper?

JASPER: How now Lord Susna!

SUSNA: Did it pass by? The creature?

JASPER: Peace Susna peace. What creature flusters you?

SUSNA: A creature in human form whose skin was a chalky white. Hair yellow like the sun. Eyes – if they were eyes – they were an unnatural blue

SPADE: Chalky white? That's the colour of maggots ploughing in the earth!

SUSNA: This chalky white I saw come off a boat down South, dressed in strange clothes. My men approached it. Seeing our drawn swords, it ran. This is a bad omen.

SPADE: How can this be?

SUSNA: You're certain no one has passed here?

SPADE : No.

JASPER: This night plays tricks on us all. For security, we must undertake a search.

SUSNA: What a sight! I'm shaking still – look!

JASPER: Knowing it has features unnatural, it can only move in the night. I'll go East. Spade search North. Lord Susna, since you came from down South, you go West. We'll meet at the Abracadabra Inn in two hours, Spade.

SUSNA: Abracadabra?

JASPER: Meet me here in two hours and I'll escort you there.

SUSNA: Is that really the name of an inn here?

SPADE: And no better in the whole of Mandragora's India will you find, I warrant.

SUSNA: My Indian eyes were first to see the sight. What an omen!

JASPER: To the search! And damn him who arouses ancient curses!
For malcontent nature shows us this night,
These are clearly not tidings of heaven's delight.

They exit to the sound of thunder.

Scene Two

The inner chamber of the Royal Palace. King MANDRAGORA sits in thought. Lord MUNSHI enters and coughs to gain MANDRAGORA's attention.

MANDRAGORA: Speak.

MUNSHI: The child is dead your Majesty.

MANDRAGORA: Its mother?

MUNSHI: Feverish. She lost a lot of blood in delivery.

MANDRAGORA: Will she live?

MUNSHI: The physicians report her final hour has dawned.

MANDRAGORA: Her final hour. 'Twas she Lord Munshi that settled the serpents that ran in my mind and tenderly groomed me to gentlemanly conduct. Her sweet voice plucked the chord of my gentler spirit; like a gardener she tended the green buds of mental tranquillity I scarce cared for.

MUNSHI: India will mourn this double loss.

MANDRAGORA: Call the Psychic.

MUNSHI: Yes your Majesty.

MUNSHI starts to exit.

MANDRAGORA: Lord Munshi? The child?

MUNSHI: 'Twas a boy. (*Pause.*) By your leave your Majesty.

LORD MUNSHI exits.

MANDRAGORA: 'Twas a boy! A son. A Prince of India! My little Prince whose life was but a wailing hiccup of breath. A sensitive soul smothered by the secret state of perpetual sleep. My rotten loins produced a poisoned seed that has taken my dear ones this night. A seed not content to ripen and bear fruit, like the evil eye it winked in my darling's womb, sprouting spider's legs that spun a web of glass in her innards. Already I hear whisperings amongst the nobles. 'He cannot produce', will they smirk politely from behind clenched lips. Men wake tomorrow to the cry of 'Father'. Now I see a serpent's egg making a pillow in my brain. Woe to the man that angers me when it's hatched.

LORD MUNSHI enters with the PSYCHIC carrying a Swastika upon whose centre sits the Koh-i-Noor Diamond.

PSYCHIC: My heart weeps for you, O Mandragora, my King.

MANDRAGORA: I called you a babbling fool, Psychic. A wandering minstrel playing an out of tune flute.

MANDRAGORA laughs slightly.

MANDRAGORA: My Koh-i-Noor diamond. What does it say?

PSYCHIC: Wake good Swastika and from thy corners breathe life,
Dance Swastika! Dance to the spirit of Earth, Air, Fire

and Water,
Awaken the Koh-i-Noor and what does thou see?

The PSYCHIC takes the Diamond and goes into a trance.
Eerie music as she speaks.

The people of India do daily toil,
Shortly the sun will perpetually boil,
A failed crop to starvation leads,
Beware the bringer of corn seeds.
Betrayal in the Court, revolt in the South,
The roars of tigers, king of predators,
A young beauty grieves her loss,
Tears that flow from a divine madness
Strange garbs and antics there be
Strange tongues that do slither towards us

MUNSHI: Please your Majesty, this is painful to the ears.

PSYCHIC: Dancing lights slice my mind!

MANDRAGORA: Continue, continue.

PSYCHIC: I am tired.

MUNSHI: We *all* are, listening to *that*. Patent those words
good Psychic, sell them at a rupee a time to the insomniacs,
why you'd be richer than all of us! Your Majesty may I
with a certain frankness speak?

MANDRAGORA: Proceed.

MUNSHI: These tails of woe and disorder trick the mind
into chaos. It's all in the interpretation. 'Betrayal in the
Court', this mystic wailed. Your Majesty's disposition is
naturally melancholic and will seek out meaning in a man's
behaviour to fit such words. The consequence being a rash
judgement of guilt where none actually exists. Words your
Majesty, mere words, yet they creep into the mind of a
King like a slow poison.

MANDRAGORA: Now is not the time to debate the issue.
Who's at Court tomorrow?

MUNSHI: Lord Susna of Madras together with…

MANDRAGORA: Susna of Madras? I see. Attend to the
Queen.

MUNSHI: By your leave your Majesty.

Exit the PSYCHIC and LORD MUNSHI.

MANDRAGORA: Susna of Madras arrives this night,
Never has he looked on me in a favourable light,
Betrayal in the Court my mystic did say,
Yet I shall see it off come what may,
My Diamond that does shine so bright,
Were thou the cause of this awful night?
Now to my Queen I shall attend,
For frightened am I she has reached her end.

He exits.

Scene Three

*The Abracadabra Inn. People are merry with drinking. A
group plays cards, someone juggles, tabla and sitar players
check their instruments. A spirit of joviality pervades the air.*

SPADE: I was born from the loins of this great place
And many a ship this port does grace
When the sun does shine on the silky sea
My heart does smile o contentedly.

EVERYONE: A child of Bombay, that am I
Proud of my birthplace till the day I die
A happy people that are we
Brave against foes and poverty.

SPADE: My mother is India and I love her so
From this fair fair land I would never go
Our culture be rich and our heritage great
A kindly race with a mighty state.

EVERYONE: A child of Bombay, that am I
Proud of my birthplace till the day I die

A happy people that are we
Brave against foes and poverty.

SUNITA: Friends! Friends! A jest to round off our song! One with meat spicier than a kebab!

Everyone laughs. Enter BINDIO.

BINDIO: A jest? A *jest?* A saucy, suggestive quip from the lips of a mere slip of a girl? A girl who is blessed with being my daughter? There shall be no jests from you, girl! Jests are for common rabble and hussies!

SUNITA: Father!

BINDIO: I brought you up the daughter of a poet – a poet, hear me, girl!

SPADE: Peace good Bindio! Tonight a Prince is born.

BINDIO: How many times have I drummed into your head,
In rhyming poetic couplets no less,
That decent girls should by now be in bed,
Or you turn my life's work into a tawdry mess!

SUNITA: Oh father, drink and be merry on this night of royal birth!

BINDIO: Drink?
Drink with the snorting,warbling common rabble,
Stoop so low that with their wit I would dabble?

SPADE: Drink Bindio – we'll eat you later.

JASPER enters. With him is a man draped head to foot in clothing, his head covered.

SPADE: Host – a fresh toddy for Jasper!

JASPER: What! Drinking Spade?

SPADE: Er, whilst waiting for you good Sir.

JASPER: We are on duty man!

SPADE: Why here's the fair Sunita good Jasper. No greeting to thy love?

JASPER: Greetings. And to you, noble Bindio.

BINDIO: He called me noble. Hear that girl? The boy sees it in the stature. It's a natural nobility Jasper, natural.

SUNITA: Sit. Come.

JASPER: I prefer my own *sober* company.

SUNITA: (*To her father.*) Prefer his own company? What is this?

BINDIO: It's the natural order of things girl. A man his own council keeps from time to time. To ponder on things past, and things possible, for the ponder yields seeds of action and action defines the man. So say the wise ones, after me. Yet there is an art in social climbing Sunita, and so I pray you climb the man with the discretion given to your female nature. He is a fine catch girl! A warrior and a Kybalian one to boot. Status dear daughter, status!

JASPER: (*To the draped man.*) Take no rash action – my sword is thirsty.

SUNITA: Is this the pondering you talked of father, for it is plain murderous, a perversion of the fabled courtesy to strangers that courses through every Indian vein.

SPADE: (*To JASPER.*) Is *this* it?

JASPER: Just as Susna described!

SPADE: Where is Susna?

SUNITA: Good Spade, cheer Jasper here,
For he sits brooding without a beer.

(*To JASPER.*) Come and talk Jasper. The night is young, the jests bad, the sack watery-weak, but rustic wit there is in abundance, and my own sweet self all for you, though, mind, no rustic am I! I have a jest that aches to be born and I believe you are its luscious father!

BINDIO: Oi! I'll pour chillies on your tongue, girl, and cake it with the mud it deserves! A daughter of Bindio talking like a harlot out of the Kama-Sutra?

JASPER: Spade, have you seen the Lord Susna?

SPADE: No.

JASPER: Cursèd be this night!

SPADE: This...creature, could it have done harm to the Lord?

SUNITA: Come come good soldier and hear my comic tale for I refuse to enter into a battle of wits with thee, 'tis against my morals to attack an unarmed person!

Everyone laughs.

SUNITA: Such a face on the man! Tell us good Jasper, what will you do when the monkey desires the return of his backside! Be merry on this night of joy my love!

JASPER: Woman has the lotus eaten thy ears? Can you not leave a man in peace! No! 'Tis not in the nature of a woman to sew her lips with honeyed thread. Like a bee must she buzz and whine until crushed by a predator. I have no interest in thy magic show, juggling tricks or silly songs. On matters of state I contemplate.

BINDIO: Insult! What a gross, unwarranted, mutinous insult!

JASPER: Old man, look in the mirror when home you tread, Does thou not realise there is no hair on thy head.

BINDIO: You baboonishly barbarous villain!

BINDIO runs at JASPER who unsheathes his sword. SPADE intervenes.

SPADE: Put up your sword Sir! Toddy is for flowering the heart, not inflaming the mind!

BINDIO: *Thou art the son of a Chinese donkey!* You insult an elder and his daughter in front of the common herd?

SUNITA: Jasper unsheathe his sword? The great Kybalian warrior – *how dare you unsheathe thy sword?*

The draped stranger looks around hoping to make an exit. JASPER turns to SPADE.

JASPER: A good eye keep on this man Spade. The visions of this night have dragged my senses to baser judgements.

SUNITA: To curse my father so! You moving stench of leprosy, go have your privates sniggered at by witless eunuchs!

BINDIO: *Sunita!*

JASPER goes to BINDIO and falls to his knees.

JASPER: Sir, I am ashamed and on my knees do beg thy forgiveness.

BINDIO: *Out of my sight donkey from hell!* Come Sunita. Never. Never – I say never again are you welcome at my house. Kybalian or not!

BINDIO and SUNITA exit.

SPADE: Let us search for the missing Lord Susna.

JASPER: The vision of this chalky white has brought me to this unseemly act. My mind be cursèd betwixt wasps and shadows. Come Spade, let us take him to Court immediately.

JASPER takes the stranger aside.

JASPER: Chalky white with thy strange eyes,
In Mandragora's hands thy fate now lies.

Exit JASPER and the stranger. SPADE follows but turns to the audience before he exits.

SPADE: Well I'll be blown how the world turns upside down and inside out! All's fair in love and war as the great Indian prophet once said and Jasper's stupid, crazy, no more than that! Ha! An insane madness it was for he has lost the fair Sunita and I shall sniff around her afresh. I too can be noble and brave. Wit counts for something these days, so the witless tell me.

He runs to bar and grabs a drink.

SPADE: A toast to the stranger unleashing passion's sin,
For on matters of love, this night my ship has come in!

He exits.

Scene Four

Trumpets or tabla sounds announce the arrival of the King. The Lord SUSNA bows.

SUSNA: My deepest sympathy your Majesty. She was an enchanting woman.

They sit at a table, MANDRAGORA at the head.

MANDRAGORA: My Queen was that, yet even in such moments the affairs of state must continue. Yesternight was full of strange acts. I understand this chalky white was captured with your help Susna.

SUSNA: The actions of mighty Jasper. We have a mighty asset in that soldier.

MANDRAGORA: Indeed. The capture of this chalky white highlights his true worth. I know not a braver man in my realm. Therefore I propose Jasper be made a Lord.

SUSNA gets up.

SUSNA: Does the King jest? This defies all ancient custom!

MANDRAGORA: Yet you admit Jasper to be a mighty asset and – I need hardly remind you – he is a member of the Kybalian Order.

SUSNA: I am very familiar with the Kybalian Order as you know! His personal nature I make no comment on. Yet his birth is common! To raise his status at this time of chaos! Was not his father a carrier of carrion who bought meat each day for your father's kitchens?

MANDRAGORA: The meat catcher reared a tiger good Susna.

SUSNA: To have equal status with the like would be intolerable. I say Madras will never have it! It's not the natural order of things. You are King of India. It is your holy duty to protect the Ancient ways not dabble in the tomfoolery of irreverent modern thinking.

MANDRAGORA: Your pleas are most passionate. So let the world remain unchanged.

SUSNA: Spoken with the wisdom of the ancients, your Majesty.

MANDRAGORA: And as we stay still surely the rest of the world moves forward?

SUSNA: Our stillness is a rock others envy.

MANDRAGORA: I believe in reward based on merit good Susna.

SUSNA: Merit is the antipathy of Kingship. When a woman chooses a man for her husband which part is true love and which the merit and status?

MANDRAGORA: Some choose for true love.

SUSNA: And others? Lo! Here comes the hero of the hour.

Enter JASPER. He bows.

JASPER: Your Majesty. Sympathy for thy terrible loss. Lord Susna, my respects.

SUSNA: How now brave one? I lost you last night.

JASPER: I was concerned for your safety my Lord.

SUSNA: The cloak of darkness convinced us to run to the Palace for safety.

MANDRAGORA: Where is the chalky white?

JASPER: Under guard.

MANDRAGORA: Bring it in.

JASPER goes to the door and ushers in the prisoner, who has now washed the mud off his skin and discarded with the turban.

SUSNA: What a sight!

MANDRAGORA: Certainly.

MANDRAGORA points to a spot near him. The prisoner walks over to the spot indicated. MANDRAGORA gets up, walks around him and then touches the prisoner's face.

MANDRAGORA: Its flesh is almost human to the touch!

SUSNA: I must touch its hair!

He does so.

SUSNA: (*Recoils in alarm.*) It's greasy! Why, it seems this creature is unaware of the art of hair-dressing! We need to send it to a hair salon.

MANDRAGORA: Let our men of science loose on this marvel! Let them measure the angle of the face, consider the ratio of nose to lips, explore skull size to determine what brain power it has.

SUSNA: All appears in order.

MANDRAGORA: Feel again the chalky white skin. Cool as monumental alabaster, it is, as if of no woman born. Is it possible it is a member of the reptilian family?

SUSNA: What a great pet this creature would be! Look at the eyes your Majesty!

MANDRAGORA: Shaped almost like ours yet devoid of almond beauty. And touched with blue as if the creature were blind!

SUSNA: I think it would make a great pet – a star attraction at Madras.

MANDRAGORA: Are you a new species of maggot chalky white?

JASPER: The King has spoken chalky white.

MANDRAGORA: Only a general perusal have I made of your report Lieutenant. It speaks?

JASPER: Indeed it does, your Majesty.

MANDRAGORA: Your name is?

THATCH: Thatch.

MANDRAGORA: Thatch! Charming! And you are from?

THATCH: Britannia.

MANDRAGORA: And where is this Britannia?

SUSNA: Near Rome to be sure!

MANDRAGORA: No! Britannia! Near the land of the Turks I would surmise! Or is it near the Afriques?

SUSNA: Maybe near those smelly Gallics! Who are they?

JASPER: The French!

MANDRAGORA: I know it now! It is that land which is the backside of France yes?

SUSNA: That's it. That land that looks like an old woman riding a pig!

THATCH: It is an island. Near the North Pole.

MANDRAGORA: The Pole! I see. That accounts for your monumentally-cool skin.

THATCH: My people are called Britannic.

MANDRAGORA: There are others?

THATCH: Indeed Sir. Britannia is populated by many that look like the snow.

MANDRAGORA: No, no, there are others that have arrived?

THATCH: There are others yes.

MANDRAGORA: And who are they?

THATCH: My friends.

MANDRAGORA: Friends.

THATCH: Yes Sir.

SUSNA: People would pay money to see the like! I want this pet your Majesty! I saw it first. He will replace my tiger.

THATCH: I am a man, Sir, and of noble birth. A lord of a place we call Lincolnshire.

SUSNA: A Lord! This chalky white claims to be a nobleman in his land!

THATCH: On my honour and the design of my coat of arms Sir. I serve my King most faithfully.

SUSNA: Your Majesty, this creature says in this land called Britannia they have a King. Imagine! A chalky white that sits on a throne!

MANDRAGORA: Logical Susna.

SUSNA: How so?

MANDRAGORA: Since they have Lords it follows there are Ladies, and thus the line runs linear to a King.

SUSNA: Your Majesty, we must treat this Lord with respect if he is indeed what he claims. Diplomacy is the right path.

MANDRAGORA: It is not diplomatic to arrive in my land unannounced. Are you an asylum seeker? If you seek asylum we shall consider it.

THATCH: I seek no asylum here.

JASPER: One other chalky white was captured an hour ago. He is held at the Guards' quarters. By the name of Jennings he pronounces himself. Grievous sick, the men of physic say his final chapter approaches.

SUSNA: Two chalky whites!

MANDRAGORA: The others?

THATCH: The noble Lord Hastings. I know not his where-abouts.

MANDRAGORA: Any more?

THATCH: Our group was one day's sailing ahead of another boat. This contained the bride-to-be of Lord Hastings, Lady Catherine of Kent, and her entourage.

MANDRAGORA: What is your purpose here?

THATCH: Many a tale has been told of the legendary land of India where the elephants do roam. Tales of vibrant colour and spice, of tigers as common as mice. Lord Hastings, being leader of our tribe proposed a voyage to become the first Britannic to set foot on this land. For twelve months at Sea we have been, fearing ourselves lost in uncharted waters until we saw your port. It was Lord Hasting's opinion to search the port in case the fair Catherine had arrived. Being separated but briefly, was I, and now I understand Lord Jennings of Buckinghamshire, captured and taken prisoner by your men. If my friend is indeed at death's door I pray you allow me to see him.

SUSNA: Your Majesty it's best to clear up the confusion surrounding the status of these chalky whites. Are they prisoners or no?

MANDRAGORA: So your purpose is a voyage of discovery?

THATCH: To explore your great country as travellers.

MANDRAGORA: So you would 'discover' us. For whose benefit, I wonder?

SUSNA: You Majesty, I would be honoured for this party to reside with us at Madras awhile. The journey itself would be a voyage of discovery for these odd looking people.

MANDRAGORA: Once the entire party of these Britannics has been accounted for by Lieutenant Jasper's Kybalian Order, you will have leave to travel India. To Madras can you go as Susna has proposed.

THATCH: I am at your mercy good Sir.

MANDRAGORA: Then let him meet with his friend just found. Keep them in comfort. Lord Susna, entertain our guests.

The Lord arises.

SUSNA: Longevity to Mandragora.

MANDRAGORA: It was nice talking to you. My mind needed a distraction.

THATCH bows. SUSNA and THATCH exit, with SUSNA inquisitively asking the stranger questions. With the KING and JASPER alone, there is a long pause.

MANDRAGORA: What say you to this?

JASPER: I like it not. There is an air of disdain that does waft about this chalky white. Odd it seems that on a whim for fanciful adventure a foreign land's gentry suddenly appear. The worm that sees an Eagle swooping ever closer does not think it flies so merely out of an inquisitive nature. There be the possibility that this be a reconnaissance.

MANDRAGORA: I know not what to think. By this Thatch's own admission there is this Hastings somewhere.

JASPER: And whether by cunning device or accidental slip this Thatch did say the fellow was their leader.

MANDRAGORA: Susna is a nosey fellow that sniffs around the coat-tails of opportunity. Better the chalky whites are with him. A good eye will he instinctively keep on them. Find Hastings and the other chalky whites.
This Tribe arrives, my Queen dies and my son breathes his first and last.
Therefore find this tribe and find them fast.

Exit JASPER.

ACT TWO

Scene One

A public garden behind BINDIO's house. Enter Lord HASTINGS. He has browned his skin with mud and covered his head with a makeshift turban from old rags.

HASTINGS: The people of this land be strange. Sullen sad small-boned sea urchins. Weak and fragile is their look. They walk with leaden shoulders carrying the weight of the world. Melancholia prospers here in the palm of plenty. My nostrils clap with glee at the thousand aromas that dance around it. I shall endeavour to pass myself as a travelling Holy Man, for I perceive the Indian mind be mighty prone to kindly acts on Holy Ones. Sweet Catherine, Lady of ladies, does thou dine with Neptune at the floor of the sea? Does thou sing with the dolphins my beloved mermaid? Will I ever again that angelic face hold and kiss? For not ashamed am I to say, Hastings his Catherine does heartily miss. Who's this coming? I'll hide to determine whether he be friend or foe.

He hides. Enter BINDIO holding a pillow and blanket followed by SUNITA.

BINDIO: Peace, I say! It's time for my siesta.

SUNITA: But…

BINDIO: Girl show me the respect that pig-ass mongrel failed to give! I will not discuss Jasper.

SUNITA: If he enters our home and offers apologies?

BINDIO: He apologised amongst that rabble and I did rabble his apology. Now leave me in peace to ripen my dreams.

SUNITA: (*Sadly.*) While mine are left to rot.

She exits. BINDIO makes himself comfortable under an apple tree.

BINDIO: Tush! The sleepy fairies call me.
    A little snoozing be good for a man
    A snoozing oozing snore for a while
     A noble man's right to sleep with nature
    I come good fairies on my daily trip
    Usual service please, a hearty little sleep
    Where my dreams be vivid as I enter the deep.

He starts to doze.

O Bindio Bindio how noble you are
Men seek your advice from near and afar
O dreamy fairies I enter thy land
This be good Bindio, take hold of my hand.

He starts snoring. Enter SPADE, holding a harp.

SPADE: Here's the old goose, resting his fat belly.

Listens to BINDIO snoring.

He makes all the saints in heaven flee with his elephant sound. This is the time to avenge myself on old Bindio for calling men like me 'common rabble'. I'll arouse his mind to the voice of the Gods. Behind these bushes to play at Gods as the fat goose sleeps.

He hides and mimics the 'Voice of God'.

Bindio! O Bindio! Can thou hear the voice?

BINDIO fidgets.

Hark, a melodious hum from this harp. O noble Bindio, most worthy of men. Noble Bindio.

BINDIO: (*In his sleep.*) What? Who's there?

SPADE: The spirit of Agni calls thee. The voice of God talks to thee.

BINDIO opens his eyes slowly.

BINDIO: How the mind plays tricks on the wise.

SPADE: Does thou hear the voice noble Bindio?

BINDIO: Who's there!

SPADE: The spirit of Agni calls thee. Bindio noblest of nobles, does thou hear the voice?

BINDIO: Noblest of nobles? I hear you spirit. What would you with me?

SPADE: Does thou hear the melodious tune?

Plays the harp louder.

BINDIO: Aye!

SPADE: Art thou attentive to the voice of God?

BINDIO: Aye!

SPADE: O Bindio! Thou art a chosen one.

BINDIO: Chosen?

SPADE: A chosen one. The spirits choose thee due to thy noble innards. Big noble innards. Chosen one, be attentive.

BINDIO: I will serve you well.

SPADE: Know you the legend of the chalky whites?

BINDIO: They are devils – maggots worming in the earth.

SPADE: Be attentive noble Bindio. If thou sees a chalky white and hears the word 'treason' bespoke thrice, then attend to the wishes of God. Attend O big innards, attend O fat one.

BINDIO: Fat one?

SPADE: Fat in nobility of mind.

BINDIO: What is it you wish?

SPADE: Does thou have the strength to execute the command of God? Great big fat elephantine inner strength?

BINDIO: Command me!

SPADE: Thus speaks the spirit of Agni. If a chalky white thou does see, and the word treason bespoke thrice, then thou art to go clad in the spirit of Agni.

BINDIO: How is the spirit of Agni dressed?

SPADE: Boots on thy feet, a fresh white loincloth…

BINDIO: What! My legs uncovered?

SPADE: And bare chested save for one piece of apparel.

BINDIO: Speak O great one.

SPADE: Thou art to wear that piece of clothing designed to control the female bosom. Wear this and think upon it for much joy lies behind it, chosen one.

BINDIO: O great one. Why am I to be dressed so?

SPADE: the wishes of Agni. Men will mock thee. O mock thee fatty! Fools will laugh at thee. But such an apparel will bring greatness to thee. This apparel must thou wear from one full moon to t'other. Does thou have the strength?

BINDIO: I do.

SPADE: Close thine eyes and rest again. Listen to the melodious tune. Sleep overpowers you…

BINDIO: Yes.

SPADE: Weariness exhausts you.

BINDIO: Mmmm.

SPADE: Sleep good Bindio. Sleep.

BINDIO starts snoring and SPADE comes out of the bushes.

SPADE: What a sight the old goose will make!

HASTINGS peeps from his hiding place.

SPADE: Now to the Palace to see the chalky white I have heard they have there.

HASTINGS: Some of my party are alive! I'll have a chat with this fellow. Good Sir! Prithee, may I chat with you?

SPADE: I'm off to the King's Palace.

HASTINGS: The King?

SPADE: King Mandragora. Don't you know that?

HASTINGS: I'm a stranger to these parts. A Holy man.

Look, see how my clothes hang on my body and my face
drips with mud.

SPADE: Follow then, the King always welcomes Holy Men.

HASTINGS: God's blessings on you my son.

They walk past the snoring BINDIO.

HASTINGS: A sounder sleeper I have not seen.

SPADE: He is at one with the Gods.

HASTINGS: Lead me to the Palace that I may bless it.
For although I be a stranger in this lovely place,
Bless it I shall, with God's Holy Grace.

They exit leaving BINDIO snoring away.

Scene Two

A hall in the Palace. Enter JASPER.

JASPER: Disturbed am I by a dream I did have
That the whole of India burned on fire
And surrounded I was by a funeral pyre.
Disease and filth polluted the air,
Men did eat flies out of sheer despair.
Disturbed I was by torches in the night,
Hissing faces that did brood with delight,
'Your King is dead', they did chant with glee
For the throne stood empty for all to see.
Yes disturbed do I be by a deathly dream,
Where goblins did hold me and I did scream.
With my arms and legs held they opened my jaw,
On the edge of my lips I did feel some claw.
'Twas the claw of a rat they held in their hands,
A disease-ridden rat with sharp slimy fangs.
Down my mouth did they push the wet black beast,
Down my throat did it run preparing to feast,
In my stomach did it sup on the food I ate,
It scratched my intestines with a smiling hate.

Biting on my lungs I did hear them burst,
Air did leave my body and to God I cursed.
The rat it wandered as I damned the Lord,
It did chew on the wire of my spinal chord,
Licking my heart with a rodent's delight,
One bite did it take and I awoke in a fright.

Laughter is heard offstage followed by:

THATCH: (*Offstage.*) This Palace is a maze of confusion and delight.

Enter THATCH laughing.

THATCH: Greetings Lieutenant Jasper!

JASPER: Lord Thatch. My condolences for the loss of your friend.

THATCH: I was glad to be with him at his final hour. This Palace is mighty impressive good soldier.

JASPER: Fitting for a King.

THATCH: Tell me good Jasper, while perusing the Palace I came across a room whose sole occupant appears to be a large diamond that sits on a crooked cross. How come that stone has such a tenancy agreement?

JASPER: Ah the Koh-i-Noor. Used by the Psychic and beloved of the King.

THATCH: A prophesying stone! What has it told the King recently?

JASPER: I don't know.

THATCH: Then let me offer a prophesy of my own. I shall twist my tongue to the strange languages I have heard in this place. I shall roll my eyes in the delivery of the speech since I have seen such a manner adopted by thy kin. Knowledge of languages is a useful tool.

JASPER: Indeed.

THATCH: Quite. Salami Aliokum!

JASPER: I beg your pardon?

THATCH: Why your greeting good Jasper! Salami Aliokum! O the joy of freedom! I was afraid you people might have cooked me for supper before my status of Lord was accepted. I tell you good soldier you would have found me tough meat.

JASPER: I see.

THATCH: On the subject of tough meat. What is this Kybalian Order that I have heard of?

JASPER: Special forces.

THATCH: Special forces! Then use such forces to find poor Lady Catherine and her entourage dear man.

JASPER: Troops continue to watch the port.

THATCH: Very good soldier. Salami Aliokum.

JASPER: Indeed. Keep practising.

JASPER exits. Enter HASTINGS wearing kurta tops and bottoms.

THATCH: Lord Hastings, the costume of this land suits you. I too may partake in the local garb.

HASTINGS: Dear Thatch, have you explored the rooms of this marble garden?

THATCH: Indeed Sir.

HASTINGS: Did you see in one a diamond most fantastic? It is like a living eye waiting to be kissed!

THATCH: A living eye indeed! Did it wink at you?

HASTINGS: Aye good Thatch.

VOICE :(*Off.*) Gentlemen, the King requests your company in the Banquet Hall.

HASTINGS: An unqualified honour. Off you go, Thatch.

THATCH: Come good Lord.

HASTINGS: I will be with you in a moment. Go to, go to.

He waits until he's left.

HASTINGS: Why it smiled and winked at me to be sure. Spoilt it was by resting on some sort of crooked cross. Separating them should be no loss. I do love that diamond I saw. After I dine with this King I will to my room, but on my way shall I make a detour.
Since this Palace is full of sumptuous heavenly bliss,
That diamond the King will surely not miss.

He exits.

Scene Three

The banquet hall. MANDRAGORA sits at the head of a table. Also seated are Lords MUNSHI, HASTINGS. All are eating and drinking. HASTINGS tastes an Indian dish.

HASTINGS: Mmm. Now *this* dish could be manipulated to serve Britannic tastes your Majesty.

MANDRAGORA: Would it not be suitable as it is?

HASTINGS: Heavens no! Extra spice would be needed to hide the true taste. Then a fitting name for the dish suitable to a Britannic ear. Why, in your honour your Majesty we could call it a Mandraloo.

MANDRAGORA: Well I wonder!

HASTINGS: Wonder! Wonder indeed! Yes I have it. *The Wonderloo!* There's money to be made in that. A traditional Indian dish created by a Britannic! *The Wonderloo!*

MANDRAGORA stands, holding a glass of wine.

MANDRAGORA: Good luck with your culinary experiments good Hastings. Noble gentlemen! The time draws near for you to depart so I must say a few words. As King of India, I am mightily pleased to meet your tribe of Britannic. I hope your travels in my land reward your minds. Madras is a great city, enjoy the journey and God's blessings to all.

They all stand and clap.

HASTINGS: Many thanks do I give your Majesty and indeed the parting bird does sing. On behalf of we Britannics I extend the hand of friendship to the land of India and to you personally for your cordiality.

MUNSHI claps followed by the others who now generally mingle apart from MANDRAGORA.
Enter BINDIO. BINDIO rushes to MANDRAGORA and kneels before him.

BINDIO: *Your Majesty! Your servant Bindio is here!* I held you in my arms while delivering advice to your great father.

MUNSHI: Bindio! How did you get past security? Get out!

BINDIO: Munshi!

MANDRAGORA: Who is this?

MUNSHI: A would-be poet your Majesty that I know from my school days.

BINDIO: What are you Munshi? Royal butler?

MUNSHI: I am Chief Council to the King of India!

BINDIO: Chief Council? Oh no your Majesty. Your father will turn in his grave! This Munshi is a dullard of the highest order. I say he is a royal butler in truth. Watch your property young King, for Munshi here with a nod and a wink is inclined to keep it! Observe closely the plates in his house, for they will have the Royal seal upon them.

MUNSHI: Get out Bindio!

BINDIO: Munshi! Upon mine honour!

BINDIO gives MUNSHI a hearty slap on the back whilst MUNSHI is sipping wine. Thus wine spills on the table.

MUNSHI: Remember where you are Bindio! Then kindly take your leave!

MANDRAGORA: Let him be good Munshi, let him be.

HASTINGS: (*To BINDIO.*) Greetings good sleeper! I espied you having quite a slumber on my way to this grand palace.

BINDIO stares at him.

BINDIO: I am certain it was no dream for here are chalky whites in front of my eyes.

MUNSHI: Drink Bindio drink, it is better your mouth fill with wine than words.

SUNITA enters. She kneels in front of the King.

SUNITA: Your Majesty. I beg apologies for the intrusion and seek only to remove my father from this place.

BINDIO: *Remove! Good God girl I have only just arrived!*

SUNITA: My father is not himself since his wits left him.

MANDRAGORA: Sweet girl, we have already dined and parting gestures given. Your father is welcome here and you are too.

SUNITA: Why your Majesty I thank you for your kindness!

She gets up and takes a drink from MUNSHI.

HASTINGS: By your leave. I retire to my room before our southbound journey.

MANDRAGORA: Safe journey Hastings.

MUNSHI: Noble Hastings, we will walk with you.

HASTINGS: In truth, I prefer my own solace. One last caress of the ambience of this place is my desire.

MUNSHI: Then at the gates shall Lord Susna himself wait for you.

HASTINGS bows and exits one way. BINDIO meanwhile watches SUNITA and MUNSHI in conversation.

BINDIO: Careful daughter – that Royal butler will steal the keys dangling from your petticoat when you're not looking!

MUNSHI: It's not treason to talk Bindio – except in your case.

BINDIO: *Oh – that word!*

MUNSHI: What is it with you? Your majesty, look how this Bindio shakes at the word 'treason'.

BINDIO: And again!

MUNSHI: Your Majesty take note at how the word 'treason' shakes the man! He must have conspiracies fermenting in his brain.

BINDIO: *I come good spirits! Thy servant Bindio shall obey!*

SUNITA: Father, what is this?

MUNSHI: Bindio, you are a fool now and were so at school.

BINDIO: I will see you anon. The spirits call me. I see them. I hear them. There is glass resting now that shines with the light of God. It is time to appoint a great hero and one amongst us desires to drink the Soma. Agni is here and sees all! Thief! There are thieves here! Agni that hides in the orb of the sun will unleash her fire!

SUNITA: Father please!

BINDIO exits.

SUNITA: Apologies your Majesty!

MANDRAGORA stands.

MANDRAGORA: The behaviour of men is strange. Sometimes I think they are like children dancing in a fairy land. Strange…

MANDRAGORA wobbles slightly and puts a hand to his head.

MANDRAGORA: Strange that men…that…men…

MANDRAGORA collapses.

SUNITA: The King falls!

MUNSHI: Look to the King! Look to the King!

Everyone rushes around MANDRAGORA. MUNSHI helps MANDRAGORA to his feet.

MANDRAGORA: Help me to my chamber good Munshi and bring the Koh-i-Noor.

MUNSHI: Yes your Majesty.

MUNSHI exits with the King.

SUNITA: My heart broke, seeing the King in such a state.
There is a pestilence in the air that will afflict us all.
I must to the chambers go,
To see if our King be well or no.

All exit.

Scene Four

MANDRAGORA's chambers. MANDRAGORA lies on a bed. MUNSHI enters.

MANDRAGORA: My Diamond, let me have it.

MUNSHI: It is not in its place.

MANDRAGORA: Then the Psychic has it. Call her hither.

MUNSHI: She left the Palace to holiday with her family yester night, but I am certain I saw the Koh-i-Noor today.

MANDRAGORA gets up.

MANDRAGORA: Susna and the chalky whites?

MUNSHI: Off to Madras, as you commanded.

MANDRAGORA: *Call security Munshi!* One of that party has stolen my Diamond. Send a party at speed to catch them.

MUNSHI: But your Majesty…

MANDRAGORA: My heart screams 'thief' when I think of the man Hastings. *Do not stand there man! A party of soldiers send out!*

MUNSHI rushes off.

MANDRAGORA: That chalky white smiled and whined pleasantries and like the bastard that mocks his parentage he has mocked me. O serpent that lives in my brain, do not hatch now for I feel your kick.

JASPER enters.

JASPER: Your Majesty, we have found a survivor from the other chalky white boat. She goes by the name of Catherine of Kent.

MANDRAGORA: Where is the woman?

JASPER: Guarded at the door here.

MANDRAGORA: Jasper, my Koh-i-Noor Diamond has been stolen by Hastings – my Diamond which I love with my life. Now you tell me I have this woman that would be the thief's wife. Bring her here!

JASPER goes to the door and enters with a tired Lady CATHERINE. He pushes her into the room. JASPER exits.

CATHERINE: What rough treatment is this! To be pushed so! I be Catherine of Kent, not some animal. Pray Sir, who art thou?

MANDRAGORA: Mandragora.

CATHERINE: What a tongue twister that be. Good Sir, let me tell thee that I am a lady.

MANDRAGORA: And I, chalky white, am the King.

CATHERINE: King?

MANDRAGORA: King of India. You are my prisoner.

CATHERINE: My crime pray tell?

MANDRAGORA: Your man Hastings has stolen my Diamond.

CATHERINE: *Hastings!* Oh, where is the love of all my sonnets?

MANDRAGORA: Your *love* as you call him is a common

thief and a most courteous liar. Off to Madras runs the swine with my Koh-i-Noor.

CATHERINE: There is not a braver man in all the world than he. A common thief he is not. You are mistaken.

MANDRAGORA: Do not strike an insolent tone with me chalky white.

CATHERINE: My name is Catherine. Lady Catherine of Kent. Notice I did not call *you* 'little brown man'.

MANDRAGORA: Vicious, viperous tongue! It is apt a swine like Hastings chooses to breed his piglets with you.

CATHERINE: What a show of emotionalism! Emotion I am told be the dominant mode of the Indian soul. As evidenced by a full-open mouth when you speak. A certain rationality do we Britannics keep in our heads, lips dainty and clipped to control the excesses of heat flowing from our mouths.

MANDRAGORA unsheathes his sword and points it at CATHERINE.

MANDRAGORA: Since the rationality in your head shows no respect to a King, then 'tis most certain your head will fall off.

Pause.

Jasper!

JASPER enters.

This woman is my prisoner. Send a message to Hastings and his tribe that we shall exchange her for my diamond. In a room place her. Gather up all the muck in the latrines and place it in her room. Then take the body of the dead chalky white and throw it in to keep her company, as she favours sealed lips.

CATHERINE: Which of my friends has died?

MANDRAGORA: The corpse will rationally tell you himself.

CATHERINE: What wicked treatment is this!

43

MANDRAGORA: It's rational. Let rubbish with rubbish live.

CATHERINE: O vile, barbarous villain!

MANDRAGORA: Take her away Jasper!

CATHERINE is manhandled out of MANDRAGORA's chambers.

MANDRAGORA: I will get even with this tribe of Britannics.
If Hastings wants this woman for his wife,
My Diamond he must return or he forfeits her life.

MANDRAGORA exits.

ACT THREE

Scene One

Three weeks later. The front of BINDIO's house. SPADE enters and approaches the front door. He knocks, waits, is about to knock again when SUNITA answers.

SPADE: Fair Sunita! For three weeks you and your father have been invisible to the world.

SUNITA: I hide my head in shame and like a nun or a woman widowed have no discourse with the world.

SPADE: Why? What shame can be so great?

SUNITA: The shame of being my father's daughter. He is not the man he once was.

BINDIO: (*Offstage.*) Who attends us daughter?

SPADE: What do you mean?

SUNITA: For three weeks he has worn, well I fear to describe it. A madness has inflicted him. I have resisted his attempts to leave this house in such a strange garb. Strange words and phrases are emitted from his mouth. such a sight. And to top it all, from his mouth come no rhyming couplets but words that carry no rhyme or reason.

BINDIO: (*Offstage.*) *Prithee girl, who attends!*

SUNITA: I am afraid to leave him in this madness and I fear my not letting him out has made it worse.

BINDIO comes to the door. He is wearing boots, white loin-cloth and a 'bra'-like top.

BINDIO: Girl I called twice. Ahh! Spade, how goes it?

SPADE: Noble Bindio…well I say!

SUNITA: Shame, thy name is Sunita! You see Spade, this madness beyond belief!

BINDIO: O spirits I do love thee!

SPADE: Bindio this be most…strange.

SUNITA: Please father, this behaviour will drive you straight to an asylum.

BINDIO: Girl you quack like a cow. Quack! Quack! Quack! My belly is hungry so cook it lunch.

SUNITA: But were you not cooking just now?

BINDIO: I was, but I have spoilt the food I was making. For the eggs fried nicely when all of a sudden the shells broke and it all become very messy.

SUNITA: Lord Shiva! I beg you Spade help me in my plight!

BINDIO: Fret not child, fret not. I have prepared a chicken. I have plucked it and stuffed it, so all you need do is kill it and cook it.

SUNITA: You see this madness good Spade!

BINDIO: I must give this dress a name! Come girl, my belly quacks. Quack! Quack! Quack!

BINDIO goes back inside the house.

SUNITA: What will happen to my father?

SPADE: 'Best he is mocked in public. This may bring him altogether again. Perhaps we can call the King's physic.

SUNITA: What will you say to him?

SPADE: That in the burning hot summer's heat,
Bindio wild mushrooms did foolishly eat.

SUNITA closes the door and SPADE turns to the audience.

SPADE: Quack goes his nobility and his madness is as wide as his girth!
For with my witty jest will I have shown fair Sunita I can move both heaven and Earth!

Scene Two

MANDRAGORA sits on this throne attended by MUNSHI and JASPER.

MANDRAGORA: Three weeks! Three weeks since the tribe of Britannics ran to Madras. From the vagabond Hastings I expected some communication since I have his woman. And this silence from Susna is deafening! Jasper, what says Secret Intelligence?

JASPER: Madras is on the brink of a mighty hunger. And a thousand spies have been sent here.

MANDRAGORA: Does Hastings not love his woman? A thousand spies! Lord Munshi, how goes it with the chalky white?

MUNSHI: She comforts herself with her holy book. She has lately become ill due to flies and maggots breeding in her room.

MANDRAGORA: Bring her here.

MUNSHI bows and exits.

MANDRAGORA: A thousand spies Jasper. Like flies and maggots. I need some one to undertake a mission to Madras. Who is prepared to die?

JASPER: Forsooth – send I your Majesty, I be willing to die .

MANDRAGORA: Forsooth? What kind of phraseology is that?

JASPER: It is the Kybalian way, your Majesty.

MANDRAGORA: Well forsooth and prithee and lo hark mark me Jasper this soldier needs to be someone who can effortlessly wear the mask of hatred to me. Susna would never believe it if that person was you.

JASPER: Then the soldier Spade could be the man.

MANDRAGORA: What is Susna's game here?

JASPER: Revenge?

MANDRAGORA: For Surongi?

JASPER: They *were* bethrothed to each other...

MANDRAGORA: And would have married had I not got in the way. I know the story good Jasper. Why all this time his restraint has been in honour of *her* and not the King at all.

JASPER: We have no proof of this.

MANDRAGORA: His silence is proof enough. Go brief the soldier and remind him this is highly sensitive.

JASPER bows and exits and Lord MUNSHI enters with a pale and ill-looking CATHERINE.

I am told you are unwell.

CATHERINE: I vomit food, and when it pours out I think of you. The stench, it reminds me of your face. When I see flies breeding maggots it brings to mind your sick self. When I see poor Jennings festering with the diseases of the dead I wish it was you! Lord Jennings in death's state has more nobility in his rotten carcass than you could ever possess!

MANDRAGORA: Lord Munshi tells me you read the Bible. Yet your tongue pours forth all that is against your faith.

CATHERINE: Chide not my Christianity. What is *your* religion?

MANDRAGORA: My religion...is India. My faith...the Koh-i-Noor and now it is separated from the Swastika. The Diamond belongs with the Cross! Three weeks have passed and your love has not claimed you – surely that is against the teachings of your Christ?

CATHERINE is silent.

If he loves you, why has he not claimed you and returned my diamond?

CATHERINE is silent.

Lord Munshi, remove the lady from her odious room. Place her in one that smells of sweet roses. Give the chalky white Jennings burial appropriate to his faith. Allow this woman to roam the gardens but under constant guard.

MUNSHI: As you wish your Majesty.

CATHERINE is silent.

MANDRAGORA: Lord Munshi, who took my message to Madras that we have this lady?

MUNSHI: A young soldier by the name of Janaka, and a great soldier I do see in him.

MANDRAGORA: Execute him.

There is a pause.

MUNSHI: Your Majesty?

MANDRAGORA: The soldier – execute him. Then send his head to Susna in Madras. Attach a note – the next one will be a female head. The stallion the soldier rode, cut off its head and I will offer it to the Gods.

CATHERINE: Have you a human heart? Where is there *justice* in this land called India?

MANDRAGORA: Munshi, carry out my orders!

MUNSHI starts to leave, taking CATHERINE with him.

CATHERINE: You are a monster Mandragora! A monster!

MANDRAGORA: I wonder if you cry for the soldier or the horse!

CATHERINE: Murderer! Murderer! How uncivilized thou art,
May justice strike thee and tear out thy heart!

Exit MUNSHI and CATHERINE. MANDRAGORA puts a hand to his head as if in pain.

Scene Three

Madras. The Palace of Lord SUSNA. Enter SUSNA and HASTINGS.

SUSNA: The corn fields rot in front of our eyes Hastings. The sun, that flagrant robber of water, will kill us.

HASTINGS: This potential famine can be avoided Susna.

SUSNA: This is a curse from God for defiance of the King.

HASTINGS: I did not take the Koh-i-Noor. Your King makes up this flimsy charge to get at *you* Susna. He uses our visitation as a tool to destroy you.

SUSNA: Do you really think so?

HASTINGS: He is not fit to be King – surely you can see that? Did he not try to make his Lieutenant Jasper a Lord? On all matters of State, has he not argued with you over the right and just way? It is obvious Susna. He hates you for he sees all the strength of character fit for true leadership abundantly displayed on your godly chest.

HASTINGS takes a pouch out of his pocket.

HASTINGS: Look here Susna. In this pouch I have corn seeds and I know best how to avoid your gloom.

SUSNA: How?

HASTINGS: Change your economic system man! It's backward to produce merely for subsistence and give in relation to need. Man needs incentive and that means profit, Susna – greed. Private greed makes public welfare. Produce by private hands and set up a market. Let an invisible hand come into play to control market forces. Susna, the key to all is desecration, desecration, desecration.

SUSNA: Desecration?

HASTINGS: Only by knowledge can this creaking carcass called India modernise Susna! Modernisation is the key man! Desecrate holy winks and kisses to the past. Let the market come and unfurl what may.

SUSNA: But what of those that rely on subsistence? The sick, the elderly and the like?

HASTINGS: Let them die Susna, let them die. No, Susna, politeness and truth do not sleep in the same bed. The lower orders are only and everywhere scum of this earth. Since the beginning of recorded time they have been an irritant. Does a clean noble lady open her legs to a beggar man's son? No! The scum of savages that wrestle below us, how they dream of entering our world, penetrating our ladies with their thistle-filled seed. No Susna. Set up a private economy. Madras shall be capital of this great land and *you* Susna, *you* shall be what you rightfully deserve to be, *King of India*. What I say may not be polite, but it is nothing but the clearest truth Susna. A New India Susna, modern, able and ready for the world.

SUSNA: Oh, what revelation is this! To speak without respect for the niceties of good manners! I will sign a proclamation ordering the implementation of your economic reforms!

HASTINGS: Commendably wise, my noble Lord. I have no reverse gear Susna, show Mandragora that neither have you.

SUSNA: He stole the woman I loved.

HASTINGS: Stole her Susna! And the swine accuses *me* of theft! How it must have tormented you imagining them in tempestuous love-making, her legs wrapped around him, two burning chariots in the night, with his seed laughing at you.

SUSNA: What Surongi saw in his melancholic demeanour I know not.

HASTING: She saw the title Queen of India.

SUSNA: And the Kybalian Order, our most elite forces have become corrupted by him. Politicised. For now they are a tool of a King rather than the State.

HASTINGS: Thus giving corrupt intelligence. This explains the whispers.

SUSNA: Whispers?

HASTINGS: Voices in the night, why on that first night in the dark of unknown streets whispers waltzed near me. I heard talk, dangerous talk pertaining to the Kybalian Order.

SUSNA: Talk from where?

HASTINGS: From alleys and sidestreets. You must surely know what I have heard?

SUSNA: No.

HASTINGS: It has come to me, don't ask me how, let's call it through the power of crystal, that Queen Surongi realized her true love was *you* Susna, and in a rage the King ordered the Kybalian Order to kill her.

SUSNA: This cannot be true.

HASTINGS: Believe it man for it is God's truth! Mandragora must be stopped, at all costs good Susna for he is simply mad.

SUSNA: I thought him melancholic and despised the peoples love for him, but mad?

HASTINGS: He is a man most dangerous Susna since his mind has left him.

SUSNA: But what of your bride-to-be?

HASTINGS: He does not have her and if he has, he intends to kill her. Therefore I have trained my mind to presume that she is dead.

SUSNA: I love the clarity of your mind.
Come my friend, let us breath life into the corn fields of Madras,
And by our success show that Mandragora is an ass.

They exit.

Scene Four

A room in the Palace. CATHERINE goes to a bookshelf and picks up a book. MANDRAGORA enters, carrying the Swastika.

CATHERINE: What brings *you* here King of Maggots?

MANDRAGORA: Are you still reading your Bible?

CATHERINE: I am not interested in polite conversation. A sickness has entered this room and I don't like the aroma.

MANDRAGORA: Tell me since you're a Christian what say you to the following. One thousand three hundred years ago – there lived Ies Christna here in India. He was a Messiah foretold by all the prophets, the son of the Holy spirit of Agni and the Virgin Maia. Christna was worshipped by the Magi, *wise men*, a brilliant star stood over the place of his birth. His doctrines have been embodied in the Puranas, a copy of which you are free to peruse. He was followed by ten disciples, persecuted and crucified on a wooden cross at the age of thirty-three.

CATHERINE: How you claim all things as being Indian! Is it merely your trait or one shared by your people?

MANDRAGORA: The Christ you worship is based on a story stolen from the land of India. Is stealing an instinctual habit of your tribe?

CATHERINE: The world is full of thieves, Indian ones too I am sure.

MANDRAGORA: Your turned-up nose is a sight to behold and for what pray tell? Kindly discard your sense of superiority into the abyss of the Hell I shall send it to. I have never found a scholar of ours that could deny that a single shelf of Indian poetry is worth the whole native literature of your rotten tribe.

CATHERINE: We do not kill innocents!

MANDRAGORA: How naïve! You stand there cradling your oh-so sophisticated manners and holier-than-thou demeanour. It's you and your band of chalky whites that are wicked, wanting to accomplish your own ends. I desire my Koh-i-Noor and since it's my property, it's not too much to ask for. Then you would be prisoner no more.

Pause as they stare at each other.

MANDRAGORA: A coldness has entered this place and it appears darker now yet there is no change in light. This Swastika without the Koh-i-Noor is like man without woman, night without day. It slowly dies and I feel its anger. The heart of it has been ripped out by a lustful greed. Do you not feel its anger and pain?

CATHERINE: I see a crooked cross held by a crooked man.

MANDRAGORA: Then you and your ilk can never see clearly.

MANDRAGORA exits.

CATHERINE: O Hastings! Why has thou taken this King's Diamond?
For 'tis clear this has caused great strife,
And I shall be made to pay with my life.

Scene Five

The Abracadabra Inn. Amongst others present, JASPER is holding a bag occasionally checking its contents.

SPADE: Good Jasper, you're checking the contents of that bag.

JASPER: Aye. The contents need checking from time to time.

SPADE: So what is in your bag?

JASPER: Chickens.

SPADE: Chickens! Let me have one!

JASPER: No.

SPADE: If I can guess how many it holds, will you give me one?

JASPER: If you guess correctly, I'll give you both.

SPADE: Six?

JASPER and the crowd in the Abracadabra laugh.

SPADE: Laughter is a wonderful thing. So other jesters tell me.

JASPER: They are polite. While they pay respects to you, they're hiding their yawns.

SPADE: Ah! This from the man that has been practicing the Sitar for near on ten years now, only to find that you don't blow it!

JASPER: How ashamed your parents would be to see you now good soldier. Do they not think you are in prison?

Enter BINDIO followed by a disgruntled SUNITA.

SPADE: Lo! What a sight!

JASPER: *Bindio?*

BINDIO: Mock me, aye, go ahead. This bosom holder is mighty useful. I shall give it a name. I'll call it the *Manzeer!*

SPADE: A glass of toddy for our Manzeer here!

SUNITA: Shame thy name is Sunita!

JASPER: Bindio, this is – highly irregular.

BINDIO: Jasper, has the King passed any law on clothing?

JASPER: No, but...

BINDIO: Then there are no buts.

SPADE: Well I see a big butt from here Bindio!

BINDIO: You may mock me. You'll answer to the spirit of Agni. Mock me, do. It proves the less people know the more stubbornly they know it.

SPADE: The more you understand the less you realise you know. Fair Sunita, Bindio's new-found personality may grow on you.

SUNITA: Yes, like warts.

SPADE: Never make love in a cornfield good Bindio, it will go against the grain!

SUNITA: These jests simply suffer my brain! My father has gone mad!

BINDIO: I am the chosen one, a noble spirit. I wear my manzeer with pride.

SPADE: Sunita, it's simple to cure Bindio of his illness. I have the knowledge. Practised I am in the dark arts of wit and the healing arts of charm. I can cure him for a price mind. Not a high price I say, but it ends with the phrase 'I do'.

JASPER: Good fellow, what nonsense is this!

BINDIO: It's the mere nonsense of the rabble. A rabble of nonsense spoken by those that possess no sense, and since no sense be *non sense* by definition it's a rabble, devoid of all articulacy and imagination. Common nonsense riddled in rabble whose structure is none but rubble that does render the riddle of the rabble from no sense to nonsense.

JASPER: Why use one word when a thousand will do?

SPADE grabs his harp.

SPADE: Prepare to be cured Bindio.

SPADE now goes into the voice he used to fool BINDIO in the public garden, playing his harp.

SPADE: Men will mock thee. Fools will laugh at thee. But such an apparel will bring greatness to thee O Bindio. *It was I hiding in the bushes!*

BINDIO: No spirit?

SPADE: *It was me!*

BINDIO: No spirit of Agni?

BINDIO looks at SPADE, stares at his daughter, looks at the audience, then his clothes, screams in horror and exits the inn. Everyone laughs except SUNITA.

SPADE: He's cured now Sunita!

SUNITA: This was your jest?

SPADE: A small one.

SUNITA: From one full moon to another I have suffered this?

SPADE: And marvellous it was don't you think? Have I not proven the spirit of the common man is as noble and active as any other?

SUNITA: By this silly jest?

SPADE: Well yes.

SUNITA: Why Spade the nobility that runs in my blood is beyond thee for a woman's heart always belongs to the man of action not the saucy jests of comic clowns.

SPADE: Saucy jests of comic clowns! We are more than some common rabble.

SUNITA: Yet the proof you claim to show is but common and coarse and I have no truck with it. You have shown you have the common sense of a carrot. You will never amount to anything having been belched forth from the rancid bowels of hell.

SPADE: But Sunita!

SUNITA starts to exit.

SPADE: I can be more than you think my love!

SUNITA: It's quite alright to be ignorant Spade, but to make a career of it!

She exits.

JASPER: It seems in love you have lost good Spade.

SPADE: Well I'll be damned!

JASPER: Yet I am, and always shall be a man of honour. For in matters of love, may the best man win. There is a chance of winning the maiden's heart again, but 'tis dangerous.

SPADE: Tell me good Sir!

JASPER: The king wants thee to go on a mission most secret. Its failure will bring thee certain death, but its success… why even the strong-willed Sunita may show a warm heart.

SPADE: Then I shall do the deed.

JASPER: Come then, that I may prepare thee soldier.

SPADE: Sunita! (*To the audience.*) Women eh? She's a tad
cross but I see her heart melting now. She'll be thinking
about me now I'm sure. I shall show her I too am a man
of action, fearless and brave!
Just think – we are all often that which we are not.
This simple truth Bindio had quite forgot.
For though we are simple souls in this boozy place,
We are also Mandragora's Indians, by God's holy grace.

Interval.

ACT FOUR

Scene One

Six months later. A room in the Palace. CATHERINE wears half Indian, half English apparel. She lights a candle, stares at the flame and puffs on a hookah. Then starts practising Kathak dance. MANDRAGORA comes to the door holding a ball and watches awhile. She suddenly stops on seeing him.

CATHERINE: (*Embarrassed.*) Kathak is a lovely dance.

MANDRAGORA: So I see.

CATHERINE: Is today the fateful day?

MANDRAGORA: For what?

CATHERINE: My execution.

MANDRAGORA: It's been six months since your man Hastings ran off with my Diamond.

CATHERINE: Six months!

MANDRAGORA: Does Hastings not love you?

CATHERINE: I don't think too much of that name now. Will the King share my hookah?

MANDRAGORA takes it and smokes.

MANDRAGORA: *In the name of the all the Gods woman!* What's in this?

CATHERINE: Is the King of India so frail?

MANDRAGORA: Lady the concoction in this hookah would be classified as illegal by my council.

CATHERINE: Come come, allow me some pleasure. It frees my mind and lets my soul fly good King.

MANDRAGORA: Such narcotics lead to delusions and madness.

CATHERINE: Dance with me. Dance the Kathak with your prisoner.

MANDRAGORA: 'Twas my Queen that loved the Kathak and when she danced it my heart was hers forever. Why for her I damned God's good grace and a Lord of Madras.

CATHERINE: Romance from the King of India, and I thought you were as romantic as a hole full of snakes!

MANDRAGORA: I fail to understand Hastings' love for you. His actions confuse me. Why does he not care for you? I have assumed Love has a universal definition, but maybe I am mistaken. Why for my Queen Surongi I did court trouble, bringing disrepute on the throne, but my passion was too great for her. I suffered a blindness for she had disturbed the royal chambers of my heart. Why it was a scandal in its day, for my actions caused tension between Crown and Lords, especially those in the South, Susna in particular, and I know he has hated me ever since. Yet Hastings simply ignores your fate when I would have fought to the last to be with the woman I loved

CATHERINE: If my life relies on him, then it's surely as good as expired.

MANDRAGORA: He deludes my people in Madras, like the hookah deludes you.

Pause as he starts bouncing the ball on the floor.

CATHERINE: What's that?

MANDRAGORA: Pig's bladder, rounded by water then dried. Making a firm sphere.

CATHERINE: Your point?

MANDRAGORA: This sphere. According to our ancient astronomer Aryabhata, the Earth is round and rotates on its own axis, thus causing night and day. He also says that the moon is dark and shines only due to the light of the sun.

CATHERINE: The Earth round! What an unnaturally silly

idea! I am reminded of your silly idea of the mechanical bird.

MANDRAGORA: The mechanical bird is also mentioned in our ancient texts. With detailed drawings on how it may work.

Releasing the ball, he takes a letter, folds it and flies it to her.

MANDRAGORA: See – like a bird.

CATHERINE: A most bizarre imagination.

MANDRAGORA: We could make a mechanical bird that could cut a swathe in the sky. Why, one day men might even reach the moon.

CATHERINE: Call the physic your Majesty, my hookah overpowers you.

CATHERINE opens the letter he has flown over to her.

CATHERINE: This mentions Hastings!

She quickly reads the letter and puts it down.

MANDRAGORA: My mind rests now on my beloved Koh-i-Noor.

CATHERINE: The letter was from an old man. He says Hastings has brought new ways to Madras, that cause him hunger, his children hunger; so too his grandchildren... Sometimes I hear a spirit call me and say "Fear not Catherine, for the King will not kill thee."

MANDRAGORA: Catherine, your hookah is narcotic and thy incoherent babbling reaches for its zenith.

CATHERINE starts to laugh.

CATHERINE: The King of India is afraid to find his inner freedom.

MANDRAGORA: I search for it without narcotic help.

CATHERINE: Chiding me again?

MANDRAGORA: Thou cackles a great deal yet I see no eggs yet.

CATHERINE: In the land of the witless, I see the half-wit is king.

MANDRAGORA: I have never been intellectually outclassed by a yapping pup.: Mark my words, too much hookah will see you kissed by the front of a marching elephant. Where is your much vaunted Britannic rationality?

CATHERINE: Your Kathak is a dance of love and I drink the milk of your aancient texts.
Eyk lavuz-e-mohabutt ka aadna ye fasana hai
Simtey to dhil-e-ashiq; pheyley to zamana hai!
A little meditation on the word love, when it contracts the heart is impassioned, when it flowers, it is the world.

MANDRAGORA: Your Urdu is impressive! Do you still love your Hastings?

CATHERINE: It would have been an arranged marriage.

MANDRAGORA: Arranged marriage?

CATHERINE: A common practice amongst our gentry to arrange their marriages based on clan, status, power and the like.

MANDRAGORA: How very peculiar your tribe is!

CATHERINE: Mighty glad am I the marriage never took place. I would prefer to be chased through the streets by a whip-yielding lunatic. Good day your Majesty!

CATHERINE exits.

MANDRAGORA: How the woman is drugged with the hookah she loves,
And now sees herself as some peace-giving dove,
Underneath that showy exterior I believe she means well,
But Susna and Hastings shall I damn straight to Hell.

Scene Two

Madras. A room in SUSNA's palace. Numerous papers cover a table.
SPADE enters.

SPADE: Now, in this witching hour between night and day, now is the time to continue my mission. I have these past six months in Madras conspired to convince Susna and his tribe of chalky whites I hate Mandragora most viciously. So now, in this hour when the ghosts leave us and the cockerel calls, such is my time to work for my King.

He goes to the table and examines some papers. As SPADE reads he hears voices offstage.

HASTINGS: (*Offstage.*) Don't worry Thatch.

THATCH: Better it comes from the people, a flow of force from below.

SPADE grabs some of the papers and hides behind a curtain. Enter THATCH and HASTINGS.

THATCH: Six months in this city was a miscalculation. We should have moved faster.

HASTINGS: The operation I plan is perfectly calculated. The people of this land are nothing short of small. I have read their inventions and seeming curiosities and the sum of their contribution to the world? The Zero. Nothing, merely nothing, a nought, only fit for playing games with crosses. Each passing day teaches me more of myself. My destiny. Good Thatch, consider. News of the economic miracle here has spread throughout the land. It is the perfect time to strike. If these people are clever, it's certainly not in economics.

THATCH: There is an art to intrigue and I fear you are missing some of its subtlety.

HASTINGS: (*Going to the table.*) Look here! Papers have been moved.

THATCH: I suspect foul play and Spade is the culprit.

HASTINGS: Why so sure?

THATCH: Stands to reason. The man was a soldier of the King, a subordinate of Jasper and the Kybalian Order. He's a spy Hastings: such is the backwardness of their intelligence-gathering they think we can't see it.

HASTINGS: We'll go to his room, interrogate him and after that, kill him. Better still, we'll go to his room and just kill him.

THATCH: Kill him?

HASTINGS: The man is a *spy*, you said. We'll tell the others he confessed before we took summary action. Come, before the others wake.

THATCH: Interrogate him only good my Lord, men such as he can be twisted again to our own purposes.

They exit. SPADE comes out from behind the curtain.

SPADE: This letter from Hastings states that the problem of India lies in its attachment to communal obligations and customs, to strange worldly beliefs that attempt to capture the cosmos which he says is the moral basis for a backward society. Interesting. Ordinarily he is insane but he has lucid moments when he is merely stupid. And in this one he defines modernisation in terms of urbanisation, literacy rates, economic freedoms, family units with two point four children… and something called performance-related pay. Time for me to leave, before Hastings's madness infects my speech.

He grabs all the papers from the table and stuffs them in his coat.

SPADE: In these papers Mandragora shall find the reason Why Susna with this tribe commits high treason.

Scene Three

Bangalore. A street. Enter HASTINGS, THATCH, SUSNA all in jubilant spirits.

HASTINGS: See with what ease we have taken this city of Bangalore, Susna!

THATCH: Look – my sword has cut many a head here! Ohm Shanti! Truth is all.

HASTINGS: Next stop – Mangalore! And then the whole South of India will be ours.

SUSNA: If Bangalore can fall so easily, so will Mangalore.

THATCH: Bangalore, Mangalore, I am Indra come again! Tu merer dihll! O India! I shall wander to the forests and remain motionless as a piece of wood in order that the great Lord Shiva appear to me. Then I shall laugh at him for such is all this nation deserves. I shall laugh and stare and laugh again and offer him a toast. Drink my seed O Shiva! Drink my seed for it is the true Soma!

HASTINGS: The heat of war intoxicates you Thatch. In honour of Lord Susna, we'll change the name of this city forthwith to Holy Susnagunji.

SUSNA: I am honoured!

HASTINGS: Today is born Holy Susnagunji. Once Mangalore is taken, the whole of the South will be land forbidden to those loyal to Mandragora. All infrastructures will be modelled on the miracle of Madras.

SUSNA: Shall we leave a fourth of our men here and strike at Mangalore?

HASTINGS: No, only a quarter – and let's strike hard.

THATCH: My Lord Hastings, will it be possible to dip in to the treasure chests of the brown-skinned ladies? It's the only advantage I see for our aggression in this sumptuous paradise.

HASTINGS: When we take Mangalore, take any woman that raises your expectation. Come, let us on with our most sacred mission.
When we unveil our new economic law,
People will look upon us in wonder and awe.

They all exit shouting and cheering.

Scene Four

A conference table. Seated are Lord MUNSHI, CATHERINE and JASPER. On a wall is a map of India with a line drawn from Madras through to Mangalore. Worried whisperings are uttered. MANDRAGORA enters. They all stand.

MANDRAGORA: They now control the chin of India.

JASPER: The line from Madras to Mangalore has been declared an exclusion zone.

MANDRAGORA: Exclusion zone? Exclusion from what ?

JASPER: Why, *you* your Majesty. They propose the idea of separate development, creating an independent southern state. For a better idea of their ways, I have this report from Spade.

MANDRAGORA: The King is waiting Jasper.

JASPER takes out SPADE's report.

JASPER: Hastings makes a case for the backwardness of our society, caused by too much attachment to communal obligations and customs.

MANDRAGORA: Constant interference by the tribe of Britannics has nothing to do with our problems of course. Pray continue.

JASPER: Another letter, this from Susna asking Hastings what be the best way to modernise Madras.

MANDRAGORA: This from the very same man that told his King not to dabble in the tomfoolery of modern thinking. Do not bore me with these love letters. What did the soldier Spade see with his own eyes?

JASPER: A land of dead noises. Clangs, grinds, knocks, raps and clatters fill the air. Even time itself has become a commodity, to be bought and sold. While some have grown rich, many suffer in poverty.

MANDRAGORA: This tribe of Britannics has infected my

people with their most rotten plague. Lord Munshi what say you to this?

MUNSHI: Their strength concerns me. If we do not accept this exclusion zone, they may attack the capital.

MANDRAGORA: I will not accept an exclusion zone.

MUNSHI: Maybe we could negotiate with Susna? Without his support, the tribe of Britannic will be illegitimate in the eyes of our people.

MANDRAGORA: No negotiation with traitors.

MUNSHI: Then we stare at being attacked.

MANDRAGORA: *Get out Munshi!* When you can offer me aggressive advice then I will be pleased to hear it. Until then, get out, for I will not hear timid talk. *I...will...not... accept...an exclusion zone!*

MUNSHI gathers his papers and exits quietly.

MANDRAGORA: Let it be known that the King has declared war on Susna and the chalky whites. What do *you* say Lieutenant Jasper?

JASPER: Our weapons are sharp.

MANDRAGORA: That's what I want to hear. Susna may have a mighty army but I have the likes of you and the Kybalian Order. I'll strike a thunderbolt at my enemies. I shall smash them to a thousand pieces, throw them to the wind and they shall be no more.

JASPER: The nature of this war must be made clear to our people. This is a war against a terror in our midst. A war against terrorism.

MANDRAGORA: I care not for the name only the victory.

CATHERINE stands and claps.

CATHERINE: Bravo! Kyar Bhat heer!

There is silence from the rest of the table.

MANDRAGORA: Catherine, you are free – I cannot spare men to guard you. You may find the town of Simla suitable to you.

CATHERINE: I'll stay here if I may.

MANDRAGORA: A very holy place is Simla. You would enjoy it.

CATHERINE: I'll visit Simla with a mind ready and willing when the time is ripe. For as your Holy Books say, not even for a moment can a man – or woman – rest without action.

MANDRAGORA: Most wise. Will you be leaving today?

CATHERINE: Today! Oh no good King for my place be here at the Palace.

MANDRAGORA: Let my gonads be bitten by a thousand angry scorpions! Prepare your strategy Jasper.

JASPER gets up, bows and exits. MUNSHI enters.

MANDRAGORA: What? Still here Munshi?

MUNSHI: Your Majesty, the Psychic is here.

MANDRAGORA: Ah, anoint my chest with such strength. Let her enter.

Enter the PSYCHIC with the Swastika in her hand.

PSYCHIC: I wish to bless you my Lord.

MANDRAGORA: And blessings I need in these dangerous times.

PSYCHIC: Remove the pollution from this room.

MANDRAGORA: Leave us.

MUNSHI: Pollution indeed!

CATHERINE and MUNSHI exit.

MANDRAGORA: The Swastika you hold good Psychic…

PSYCHIC: Cries in pain.

MANDRAGORA: This happy symbol of peace shines malignant without the Koh-i-Noor.

PSYCHIC: Malignant, maligned, maimed and murderous Mandragora. It is intoxicated by its own rage, for without the Diamond it will not survive.

MANDRAGORA: Then what is to become of us! Help me good Psychic!

MANDRAGORA kneels. The PSYCHIC takes a pouch out of her coat pocket. From it she takes a candle which she lights and makes circular motions with it around MANDRAGORA's head.

PSYCHIC: Close your eyes that I may bless you! Palms together! Fire burns now, nature's hothead, burning like a passionate heart.

MANDRAGORA: My heart is empty...

PSYCHIC: Silence.

She blows the candle out. The PSYCHIC takes some earth, makes a cup of MANDRAGORA's hands and then places the earth in them.

PSYCHIC: Earth is in your hands. It has been blessed by holy ones. Let some fall to the ground.

MANDRAGORA lets some fall.

PSYCHIC: Earth has fallen, may it bring a fresh rebirth.

The PSYCHIC takes a vial of water from her pouch. She pours some on MANDRAGORA's head.

PSYCHIC: Water, God's purest juice has anointed thee. Fire, Earth, Water, three points of the Swastika, now all points join together with Air. Close thine eyes.

MANDRAGORA closes his eyes again. The PSYCHIC proceeds to take out a dagger.

PSYCHIC: You shall feel Air and thus the four points of the

Swastika are honoured. You shall feel the Air, hot and fast from one heart to another, Mandragora, King of India.

During the last moments of the PSYCHIC's words MUNSHI enters the room. On seeing the dagger raised...

MUNSHI: Your Majesty, I intrude yes, but to be called *polluted...*

He starts to exit. MANDRAGORA opens his eyes and instinctively moves to protect himself.

MANDRAGORA: Wait! Munshi!

MANDRAGORA is stabbed in the arm. MUNSHI rushes over and attempts to overcome the PSYCHIC.

MANDRAGORA: *Help! Jasper! Help!*

PSYCIC: *How could you lose the Koh-i-Noor!*

MUNSHI and the PSYCHIC still struggle as JASPER rushes in. He manages to disengage the dagger and quickly overpowers the would-be assassin.

JASPER: Your Majesty! You are hurt!

MANDRAGORA: Superficial.

PSYCHIC: *Will be permanent next time, and that time will come!* You need to be lucky all the time, we need luck but once. You are a *traitor!* A traitor foolish enough to lose the Koh-i-Noor!

MANDRAGORA: Get her out!

JASPER exits with the PSYCHIC who shouts.

PSYCHIC: Remember remember in Mandragora's reign, The Koh-i-Noor was lost to India's shame!

MANDRAGORA: Why did you return Munshi?

MUNSHI: I came to apologise for my show of weakness. Are you in pain my King?

MANDRAGORA: It's nothing. ...

MANDRAGORA notices that MUNSHI is bleeding from the chest.

MANDRAGORA: Munshi, Munshi, you are bleeding my Lord!

Lord MUNSHI falls to his knees, MANDRAGORA rushes over to him and holds him.

MANDRAGORA: *You are bleeding most profusely!*

MUNSHI: I did feel a certain coldness in my struggle with her.

MANDRAGORA: Speak not good Munshi, speak not.

MANDRAGORA turns and shouts.

MANDRAGORA: *Help! Anyone! I need help here!*

MUNSHI: I love you good King. *You* are the son I never had.

MANDRAGORA: Don't speak.

MUNSHI: Ever since you were a twinkle in your mother's womb, the son I never had! *Your Majesty!*

MANDRAGORA: Aye noble Lord close your eyes and rest good Sir for the King holds you tight,
And this heinous act I vow to make right.

ACT FIVE

Scene One

BINDIO's house. JASPER enters and knocks on the front door. SUNITA opens it.

JASPER: Greetings my sweetheart-hidden-from-view.

SUNITA: Good Jasper.

JASPER: I come, my dearest heart to say goodbye.

SUNITA: Goodbye?

JASPER: Aye, for India is at war with the tribe of Britannics and other traitorous rebels.

SUNITA: India at war. When a woman's heart belongs to a soldier, this is a moment she prays for.

JASPER: Pardon?

SUNITA: For now I get to play the martyred bride.

JASPER: Then does your heart truly belong ?

SUNITA: Yes?

JASPER: To a soldier?

SUNITA: Yes!

JASPER: But dare I ask which?

SUNITA: Do you dare?

JASPER: I come Sunita to well, you see, I wonder, there is something...

SUNITA: Speak Jasper! Why is your tongue in a tie when only now it was loose?

JASPER: On my return, well!

SUNITA: Speak my love, and whisk my heart into cream.

JASPER: Well, how is your father?

SUNITA: My father?

JASPER: Better I hope? No more strange antics?

SUNITA: See for yourself. *Father! Good Jasper is here!*

JASPER: Did you *have* to shout?

SUNITA: Then speak before his ears regain their normal hearing.

JASPER: Fair Sunita, I am come here, clutching this rosebud in hand...*well my word I could do with some toddy!*

BINDIO comes to the door.

BINDIO: Ah Jasper! What, no rustic soldiers in your train?

JASPER: Alone as the day I was born, Sir. You are well I see.

BINDIO: Oh yes. I'll get my revenge on that ruffian Spade. I am already plotting the deed. For I have learned more about less and less, and now know everything about nothing.

SUNITA: Lieutenant Jasper is off to war.

BINDIO: Inevitable. I did see it in their eyes, cold chalky white eyes. Go brave Kybalian, go. The King mustn't be kept waiting.

JASPER: I wonder Sir, if I could have your permission – your permission, as it were Sir.

BINDIO: Permission?

JASPER: Well, *permission* Sir.

BINDIO: Ahh! I see! You like my creation?

JASPER: Like? I should say that's too weak a word – love, adore, worship, would be true to the mark!

BINDIO: Then let's agree a price without further ado.

JASPER: My word you're frank. I had not thought about the finances.

BINDIO: For you, two rupees a go.

JASPER: What!

BINDIO: There are two cups, you know. Surely the military budget will stand a trifling two rupees?

JASPER: I care not what others think!

BINDIO: Splendid! I see you in a gold-plated one!

JASPER: Gold-plated what?

BINDIO: Manzeer. How many shall the army need?

JASPER: I come not for Manzeers!

BINDIO: Good for the price – great protection I'd say.

JASPER: I come for…

BINDIO: Have you been drinking good Jasper?

JASPER: Heavens no!

BINDIO: Be off then. Men like I am destined to drink at the fountain of knowledge, others just gargle. Go to, good soldier, go to.

BINDIO shuts the door.

JASPER: As a soldier, many battles have I fought, yet asking a father for his daughter's hand takes more strength than I thought.

Scene Two

Mangalore. The city's main building is now the headquarters of HASTINGS and company. Enter THATCH carrying a bloody sword and pulling up his breeches.

THATCH: Oh you luscious Indian beauties. A delight to share my seed with you that we may beget a new race.

SUSNA enters.

THATCH: Ohm Shanti, namaste Susnaji.

SUSNA: Lord Thatch, where is the girl I saw you with?

THATCH: Girl? What girl?

SUSNA: I did see you with her good Sir!

THATCH: *Oh her!*

He points to his bloody sword and starts giggling.

THATCH: No matter. Re-incarnation shall bring her back as a monkey!

SUSNA: She was but a child!

THATCH: And she died a woman good Susna.

He places his hands on his crotch.

THATCH: Oh what a woman!

SUSNA: But she could not have been more than ten years old!

THATCH: A nation of children good Susna. Why what a marvellous nursery this country is!

SUSNA: Hastings is looking for you and this act my Lord, this most vile act...

THATCH: Chupkar! Sumji! Chupkar!

HASTINGS enters.

HASTINGS : Greetings Gentlemen.

There is general tense greetings.

THATCH: You were in search of me?

HASTINGS: I was good Thatch, I was. Gentlemen, I had a vision last night. Aye, it was like my mind had been turned into a diamond and dancing lights shone from it. I see men as the children of God, but not until yesternight did I realise what it meant. God wills our actions and God works through us. I tell you good people, I feel the hand of history on my shoulders. It is destiny that men like us shall rule this land, not only Britannics, but believers like Susna too. We shall bring order to this Indian chaos. What I am about to say will come as a shock to those of you that have known me a great time. Great sages are destined to wander in cold winds and I am such a sage in this howling wind called India. Gentlemen, I am Moses. Moses come again to lead my people. I have come back in the shape of this man Hastings, but I am Moses and once again shall I part a Red Sea. For individualism must run rampant in this land, to set the people free! We shall march on the capital tonight and strike off the crown from Mandragora's head. Praise be to God for you are moving down the road to Damascus and straight on to greatness.

There is a pause.

SUSNA: I know not of this Moses.

HASTINGS: Have faith Susna, have faith.

THATCH: I for one am a believer Hastings.

SUSNA: Some acts we commit seem to go against nature.

HASTINGS: From doubt will come certainty. I promise thee that. Come Gentlemen, let us gather our men, for Bombay does call, and destiny too!
Stay or go, 'tis up to thee,
But for the glorious path, I say follow me.

They exit.

Scene Three

The Royal Gardens. Sunset. MANDRAGORA is looking at flowers. JASPER enters.

MANDRAGORA: How is Lord Munshi?

JASPER: No change, he has descended into a coma.

MANDRAGORA: He fights this fever like a tiger. How I misjudged him. I'll always be indebted to him.

JASPER: Your Majesty, the enemy is on the road to us. The city of Miraj is close by and on the enemy's route.

MANDRAGORA: *Miraj!* An appropriate name Miraj. My

mind has wandered numerous subterranean hells hoping this whole episode is some strange nightmare, some mirage of the mind.

The sound of a gazal is heard.

MANDRAGORA: Ye Gods! Do you hear that Jasper!

JASPER: Aye.

MANDRAGORA: Queen Surongi! I hear you spirit of my beloved wife! My love, let me see you!

CATHERINE enters. She stops singing. MANDRAGORA and JASPER are speechless.

CATHERINE: Your Majesty I must speak to you.

MANDRAGORA: Not now Catherine – it's sunset, a dangerous time.

CATHERINE: I have found a suitable way to help.

MANDRAGORA: You can't be at the battlefront woman.

CATHERINE: I will attend to the wounded, the maimed, the sick and the dying. In Britannia I studied the art of *nursing.*

MANDRAGORA: No Catherine, your life would be in danger. Go to Simla, I'll find a Kathak partner for you – maybe the fair Sunita if she is willing.

CATHERINE: Will you stop being a mattress-soiling cause of wailing and gnashing of teeth! I'm become Shakti, the Spirit of Indra!

MANDRAGORA: Catherine, you'll love Simla! Please do not prove my view that there be no limit to Britannic stupidity.

CATHERINE: Tending to the sick and wounded could be organised your Majesty, and such organisation would help.

MANDRAGORA: *This is preposterous!*

JASPER: Your Majesty, consider this. We're outnumbered. Good organisation would free soldiers for battle. It could unnerve the tribe of Britannia, and Hastings in particular.

If we are destined to lose, this woman is dead anyway.

MANDRAGORA: Then to battle will you go Catherine.

JASPER: I shall check again on Lord Munshi.

JASPER bows and exits. MANDRAGORA stares at CATH-ERINE.

MANDRAGORA: Why do you really wish to be at the front of battle Catherine?

CATHERINE: To help.

MANDRAGORA: Could the name Hastings be partial reason for this desire? Maybe there's still a flickering flame of love in your heart for this man?

CATHERINE is silent.

MANDRAGORA: What will you feel when you see him?

CATHERINE: That is difficult to say your Majesty.

MANDRAGORA: Such is the way of love Catherine. It makes the sensible behave irrational, it gives blind fury to the most gentle, it is Life's deadliest disease that renders its victims useless, such is its way. Great poets have attempted to unlock its mystery, none has truly succeeded. It fascinates us, bores us, worries us, consumes us, tires us, even kills us. It is at once real and as transitory as a dream.

CATHERINE: O how I wish I could summon the trees and snakes of this earth to wrap a garland of skulls around my foolish Britannic brethren!
Humm wahaan hain jahaa se humm ko bhi,
Kuchh hamaari khabar nahin aati.

MANDRAGORA: *I am in that oblivious state, a stranger to myself wherever I am.* Is that your hookah talking?

CATHERINE: My past is but a retinue of ghosts for I have been swallowed in God's mouth and reborn anew. My heart beats like a celestial nymph swimming in an ocean of gems, climbing mountains that glow in the dark, and eating herbs that will transform me into a bird. A dove of Peace and Love!

CATHERINE cuts a jasmine flower and hands it to MAN-DRAGORA.

CATHERINE: Take this. It may be *you* that will die in battle. So take this Jasmine flower and content is my heart that at least some token I gave you. For if I spy you as I wander in the woods with my axe tending to the wounded, I will know that beneath thy seeming melancholia I see a wisdom beyond thy years.

MANDRAGORA: There is a place called Darjeeling. It's full of mystic men, go there. You'll be safe there.

CATHERINE: Certainly. After I have tended to the sick and wounded of war.

There is a pause. JASPER returns.

JASPER: Your Majesty.

MANDRAGORA: What?

JASPER: Your Majesty...Lord Munshi is dead.

MANDRAGORA unsheathes his sword.

MANDRAGORA: Now Jasper the time has come. Go, prepare for battle for we leave for Miraj tonight and wait the day of reckoning. Let us hope the Gods look kindly on us and let justice be done though the heavens fall.

JASPER exits.

MANDRAGORA: For this is, and always shall be, the land of the Koh-i-Noor. We shall go on to the end. We shall fight at Miraj, we shall fight here in Bombay, we shall fight on the seas and the oceans, we shall fight with growing confidence and growing strength, we shall defend our India, whatever the cost may be. We shall fight in the fields and in the streets, we shall fight in the hills, for we shall never surrender. For now, the Battle of India is about to begin. Upon this battle depends the survival of Indian civilisation. Upon it depends our own Indian life. Hastings will have to break us or lose the war. If we can stand up to him all India may be free and the life of the world may move forward into broad sunlit uplands where the Koh-i-Noor can shine bright. But if we fail, the whole world will fall into a Dark Age. Let us therefore brace ourselves to our duties, and so bear ourselves that, if the Indian Race and Civilization last for a thousand years, men will say, 'This was their finest hour'.

Exit CATHERINE and MANDRAGORA.

Scene Four

Miraj. The battlefield. There is mist in the air. Noise of fighting can be heard. JASPER enters covered in blood.

JASPER: *One final push good soldiers! One final push for King and Country! They have misjudged us good Indians! They have assumed victory would be sweet, but our hearts roar with the war cry and we coat ourselves with the flames of war like a blanket in a cold night such as this! Push on good soldiers! Push on!*

JASPER exits. Enter SPADE with a noose around his neck followed by THATCH holding the other end of the rope. THATCH looks around and sees a tree.

THATCH: Here will do.

SPADE: I ask thee for mercy chalky white!

THATCH: Mercy? That's a Gallic word for thank you. My pleasure. Let your Kybalian Order see your body dangling from this tree!

He throws the rope over the tree and starts making preparations to hang SPADE.

SPADE: I trust even you chalky whites give last requests.

THATCH: Juldi juldi berfkurf!

SPADE: Yes Sir. I pray to God, I say forgive me Lord Shiva for having ideas above my station, for surely such has got me into this mango pickle. Fair Sunita, if my voice could be carried by the birds to sing to you, then let them sing you my love and give you my blessing, for I thought my actions might make thee see that I am more than a mere nought.

THATCH: Have you finished?

SPADE: It's most strange Sir, I don't know what else to say.

THATCH: And this Sunita, the woman that you love?

SPADE: Aye Sir.

THATCH: In Bombay?

SPADE: Daughter of the poet Bindio Sir.

THATCH: Then I shall enter her and leave my seed inside her, on your behalf of course! Salami Aliokum.

SPADE: I beg your pardon?

THATCH now attempts the hanging but the rope snaps. SPADE falls unconscious to the ground.

THATCH: Blast if that's not the Indian rope trick! Best simply to cut off his ugly head.

THATCH unsheathes his sword, places it on SPADE's head. JASPER enters.

THATCH: Mark the timing of the Kybalian Warrior!

JASPER: How brave to strike a man while he's down. Britannic rules of engagement?

THATCH: Dirty looking Indian filth, let us exchange feelings of mutual love!

JASPER: I hope you believe in God, for you are about to meet him.

They fight. In the melee SPADE starts to stir to consciousness. JASPER notices his movement. The mist rises.

JASPER: Good Spade! Strike here for I have the fiend!

THATCH: Pern Chor!

SPADE: Why! Is this Nirvana? Pray let it be so.

JASPER: Strike Spade!

SPADE: Jasper? Art thou dead too!

JASPER: Take thy sword and strike while the iron is hot soldier!

SPADE: Sweet Sunita! I'm still flesh and bone! Here I come good Sir!

He takes his sword and starts to strike in the mist.

SPADE: All I see is mist!

JASPER: Strike now good soldier!

SPADE: Aye Sir!

He strikes and runs his sword through JASPER. THATCH escapes.

SPADE: I got him Jasper! Sir? I think I got him! Good Jasper please call!

SPADE wanders in the mist and exits crying out 'Jasper, noble Jasper'. HASTINGS enters and sees the dead body of JASPER.

HASTINGS: Such a sight brings merriment to my eyes. He is dead! The man Jasper be dead, let all the Kybalian Order know this! Moses has parted him from this life!

Enter CATHERINE holding an axe.

HASTINGS: O my soul's delight, who I had lost all hope of ever seeing! Look there! I have killed the mighty Jasper! No mirage this but actual, provable fact!

CATHERINE: You – fiend from Hell!

HASTINGS: Catherine! It's me – Hastings! Catherine? Is it really you?

CATHERINE: I am the avenging nurse of this forest. Caught betwixt the battle of two raging armies, armed with only my Hippocratic oath.

HASTINGS: Catherine! It's I! Hastings! There lies that Kybalian Jasper. Killed in mortal combat. With your axe, swiftly – cut off this man's head that I might brandish it for all to see.

CATHERINE: The man is dead. Murgia! O Jasper, murgia!

HASTINGS: Cut off his head, Catherine.

CATHERINE: Humm wahaan hain jahaa se humm ko bhi, Kuchh hamaari khabar nahin aati.
When I squat in a thoroughfare, who dare bid me away!

HASTINGS: Catherine I beg you do as I command and do it quickly!

CATHERINE: *You have spilt Indian blood.* Sarlar berfkoof! Chor!

HASTINGS: Then with my own sword will I do it.

CATHERINE prevents HASTINGS approaching JASPER by brandishing her axe.

HASTINGS: I have no quarrel with you Catherine! Leave me to carry out the deed, for I need his head. I am Moses woman! Get out of my way!

CATHERINE: *Once again I say no to this.* Pargall! Pargall! Pargall and chor!

SUSNA enters, tired and wounded.

SUSNA: Hastings! time for us to leave! *A most serious offensive has been launched against us. Many men have we lost.*

HASTINGS: But there lies the body of mighty Jasper. Without him, our victory is assured.

SUSNA: We have no time to debate and must run for our lives.

HASTINGS: Who has led this offensive against us?

SUSNA: The King himself.

CATHERINE: Kya bhaat hai! Praise be to the King! Long live India!

She rushes towards them. To save himself HASTINGS pushes

SUSNA in front of him and SUSNA takes the blow from the axe and falls to the ground. HASTINGS runs off with CATHERINE in pursuit. The background noise of battle has subsided slightly. MANDRAGORA, weak and tired, enters.

MANDRAGORA: I feel the pulse of the Koh-i-Noor close by!

The King sees the body of JASPER. He goes to JASPER and holds him in his arms.

MANDRAGORA: Know this spirits of the forest, I hold greatness in my arms. I loved this man like an elder brother. *Noble Jasper!* Here lies blood that is as Royal as mine own, our most precious blood, that has given his life for his King. Look how in Death he smiles at us.

Off-stage shouts of victory.

VOICE: (*Off.*) The battle is over. The enemy flees. India is saved.

MANDRAGORA goes to his knees and looks to the heavens.

MANDRAGORA: Thank you!

HASTINGS rushes in, chased by CATHERINE. Seeing MANDRAGORA, HASTINGS comes to a dead stop.

HASTINGS: I've taken a Kybalian, and now for a King

CATHERINE kneels.

CATHERINE: I have chased this goat to your sword your Majesty.

MANDRAGORA: And justice is coming good Catherine. Just you and I now Hastings. For Justice I intend to issue personally here.

MANDRAGORA charges at HASTINGS

MANDRAGORA: My Koh-i-Noor!

They fight, MANDRAGORA fells HASTINGS but has not killed him.

MANDRAGORA: Where is my Koh-i-Noor?

He starts to shake HASTINGS.

MANDRAGORA: Where is my Koh-i-Noor?

HASTINGS: Here in my pocket. Take it and damn you! Damn you to hell!

MANDRAGORA searches his pockets, CATHERINE helps but to no avail.

HASTINGS: I swear it was here! Please don't kill me! I swear...Thatch! Why that knave has stolen it!

MANDRAGORA: You, I shall make suffer. Your fate is a slow death. Here by this tree is your journey's end. You are bleeding profusely, let the vultures take the rest, let them take you alive. Come good nurse.

MANDRAGORA and CATHERINE take HASTINGS to the tree. MANDRAGORA sees the rope left by THATCH.

MANDRAGORA: Tie him well. Let our enemies see him in such a sorry state.

HASTINGS: To kill Moses? It is not in the scriptures.

MANDRAGORA: Babble on, I care not. I feel lost in a wilderness not of my making. For my beloved Koh-i-Noor still rests in alien hands souring this our Indian victory. When an unclean hand holds the Koh-i-Noor, it is nothing but a diamond. Seeing it as such, what will the Britannics do with my life stone? It will shed tears of light and they shall marvel at its brightness and treat it as a mere bauble, albeit the largest diamond ever seen. I shall chase this tribe over all the Earth before such a nightmare vision encroaches us. Come, let us continue the search, for my Koh-i-Noor does cry for me and I hear its pain. Gather the navy. We will re-trace the course Hastings took across the seas and land in his Britannia! Arm the ships, we set sail anon!

They exit the stage. Lights fade. From the darkness two figures appear and the lights fade up to reveal BINDIO and SPADE downstage. THATCH also enters, upstage, hiding from view.

BINDIO: Who goes there?

SPADE: Who asks?

BINDIO: Villain! You dare ask the king's loyal subject questions?

SPADE: Put up your sword!

BINDIO: Good Spade your games of folly will get you an untimely death.

SPADE: At least you joined this conflict at the right time, just at the end! You lose your honour but keep your life which I suppose be a fair exchange.

BINDIO: The wisdom of age, good Spade – never rush in when the chance for cool heads hangs by. Such is the way to play the game Spade, for the death of Munshi creates the vacancy of Chief Council to the King and I am determined to occupy it.

SPADE: Come, then, help me continue the search for the chalky white Thatch, there is a ransom on his head, a King's ransom at that!

HASTINGS: (*In a snake-like whisper.*) Help me! Help me!

They exit leaving THATCH to come downstage. From his pocket he takes the Koh-i-Noor, stares at HASTINGS, then turns to the audience.

THATCH: Hastings, you were a good thief, but I the better pickpocket. (*Looking at HASTINGS.*) What shall we do with thee, you wretched crystal castaway!

HASTINGS: In the name of God help me before I bleed to death.

THATCH: Best to head for Britannia, but avoid the ports and travel further north first hiding in the caves. Easy to fool these people with mud on the face! The sheer brightness of the beast, why it does hurt my eyes to look at, and to hold it is to love it, and to love it…to love it. This diamond shall be my fortune. The name Mandragora, why I curse it and we shall erase it out of history leaving it to wander in an eternal wind. On a Royal Britannic head shall this stone be laid down, and truly it shall be our Jewel in the Crown.

THATCH looks at HASTINGS, laughs and exits.

HASTINGS: (*In a snake-like whisper.*) Help me...help me...

Lights fade to black.